The Other Face of God

The Other Face of God

When the Stranger Calls Us Home

Mary Jo Leddy

ORBIS BOOKS
Maryknoll, New York 10545

Second Printing, April 2012

Founded in 1970, Orbis Books endeavors to publish works that enlighten the mind, nourish the spirit, and challenge the conscience. The publishing arm of the Maryknoll Fathers and Brothers, Orbis seeks to explore the global dimensions of the Christian faith and mission, to invite dialogue with diverse cultures and religious traditions, and to serve the cause of reconciliation and peace. The books published reflect the views of their authors and do not represent the official position of the Maryknoll Society. To learn more about Maryknoll and Orbis Books, please visit our website at www.maryknollsociety.org.

Manufactured in the United States of America.

Library of Congress Cataloging-in-Publication Data

Leddy, Mary Jo.
    The other face of God : when the stranger calls us home / Mary Jo Leddy.
        p. cm.
    ISBN 978-1-57075-910-9 (pbk.)
    1. Church work with refugees—Canada.   2. Romero House (Toronto, Ont.)   I. Title.

BV4466.L44 2011
261.8'328—dc22

Excerpt from "The Waste Land" from COLLECTED POEMS 1909-1962 by T.S. Eliot, copyright © 1936 by Harcourt, Inc. and renewed 1964 by T.S. Eliot. Reprinted by permission of Houghton Mifflin Harcourt Publishing Company.

Excerpt from A Timbered Choir by Wendell Berry, copyright © 1998 by Wendell Berry. Reprinted by permission of Counterpoint.

for Jack Costello, S.J.
at seventy
who walked through these pages

CONTENTS

INTRODUCTION

If you ask me, as if your life depended on it, do you believe in God? I would think twice and answer: Yes, I do believe because I have seen the face of a young woman and her name is Teresita Cedillos.

If you turned to me and asked me whether it was possible to be faithful, I would see that you have seen too much to be sure of that anymore. I would look at you and say that fidelity is real because I have known a woman who has struggled for twenty years to bring her husband home. Her name is Hidat Mosa.

If you held my hand and whispered, wondering if we could change, I would place my other hand over yours and say: Yes, because I was changed when I met a black woman with a white leg and a man who slept with his briefcase. Her name was Deequa, and his name was Gugan.

If you sat beside me and mused whether life could be meaningful, I would look ahead and say, for sure, as sure as I know the name of Osman Omar and Clara Alvarez who hung on for dear life.

If you looked me in the eyes and challenged us both about our impossible dreams for justice and peace, I would say, yes, dream on, for there is a little street called Wanda Road where strangers sometimes become neighbors.

1

If you pursued this challenge and asked whether I had seen the evil in the world, I would answer, yes, but that it had no name and no face.

If you folded your hands into prayer and intoned a most ancient question, do you believe in Jesus Christ? I would cross my heart and say, yes, because a Muslim sheik helped me help a dying man in the middle of the night. His name was Sheik Mohammed.

If you wrung your hands and asked, what about the Church? Can we be faithful as scandal piles upon scandal? We must, I would reply; that is what I learned from a man by the name of Augustin who survived the Rwandan genocide.

If you breathed deeply and asked the question that had been on your mind from the beginning, have you seen the face of God? I would reply yes.

Almost.

Always.

Teresita, Hidat, Deequa, Gugan, Osman, Clara, Sheik Mohammed and Augustin—these are some of the strangers with foreign names who have guided me on a new path toward God. As I repeat their names, like beads on a rosary, I see their faces, and I remember the first time I saw them and knew that I had been faced. Over these past twenty years, these and many others have summoned me to become myself. Strangers and foreigners, who are also called refugees, they have given me the blessing of newness, a new way of seeing the culture I live in and a new way of being in the church where my faith has been planted. They have shown me the other face of God.

The linked stories and thoughts that follow are reflective ripples out from this foundational experience. I have not attempted to set them in stone in a systematic fashion. Description often seems more appropriate than definition when a new experience stretches our former categories of thought to a breaking point.

The refugees who have become my neighbors are now the eyes of my eyes and the ears of my ears. With them, I have discovered the burden and the blessing of my own calling as a human being and as a Christian.

Where you live determines what you see. The people you listen to affect what you hear.

We met each other at Romero House, a community of service that is named after Archbishop Oscar Romero of El Salvador, a man of the church who gave his life for the poor. Romero House is actually four houses and a little storefront center in a very small neighborhood in a large metropolitan area of several million people. It is located in the west end of Toronto, the most multicultural city in the world. Our daily life and work take place within a small pie-slice-shaped neighborhood called the West Bend. It is here that we, the settled and the newcomers, the rooted and the uprooted, live and move and have our being. It is here that the local and global realities meet in very real ways. It is here that the personal and the political collide and connect. It is here that the anguish of distant lands meets the domestic sufferings of middle-class residents, and it is here that we are building an unlikely neighborhood together.

My reflections begin here, but they are meant for others

who may live very different lives in other places. I have written this book within a certain neighborhood, together with people called refugees and with the young interns who offer a year or two of service for the privilege of welcoming strangers. However, although I wrote this book with them, I did not write it for them. This book is written for those who have been shaken by the sight of someone new and different, who have summoned them to newness—to a new way of being, a new way of faith, to a new way of becoming church. This book is written for everyone for whom the experience of something or someone really new is both threatening and promising.

The newcomer may be a refugee but may also be a baby, your child, your old friend who has become quite different, your spouse whom you no longer recognize. The newcomer doesn't quite fit into our old ways of thinking and being. Same old, same old.

All too often we want to bring this newcomer into the fold of the familiar. We want to discover all the ways in which we are similar. When a child is born, we search for family resemblances. We mean it as a compliment to tell parents that the child looks like them, talks like them. We think we are quite liberal when we discover the things we hold in common with someone from another culture. After all, we are all human. These are attempts to diminish the differences between us. Thus, we domesticate the terror of the unknown and unfamiliar.

In the case of immigrants and refugees, we develop programs that will help them fit in to our culture. Our criteria for accepting immigrants are based on an assessment of those who will become a functioning part of our society. The more they fit in, the more acceptable they become.

All these efforts to fold the ones who are new and different into the file of the familiar are deeply embedded in our culture. We who live in an imperial culture, the American empire, are all too tempted to make the rest of the world "like us." Even if we have no desire to subdue other nations, we have subtle expectations that our language, our currency, our pop culture will set the standards for the rest of the world. It is this imperialism of "the same" that is now being so deeply questioned in many parts of the world. This is the totalizing worldview that has been so profoundly rejected by a wide variety of postmodern thinkers.

The Familiar Face of God

This cultural tendency to enfold what is different into what is familiar also affects our spiritual attitudes and shapes the various images we have of God and the church. We are tempted to create an image of God who is friendly and familiar, who is like us. This becomes a domesticated and manageable God who can be called upon for all kinds of personal and political solace. Such a God is thoroughly predictable and totally lacking in surprise.

This is also the God who can be called upon to protect us from strangers, those not like us, other cultures. Such a friendly God is a very useful ally against our various enemies.

We live in a time and place where we fear strangers and foreigners rather than welcome them. *They* are a threat, a danger to our way of life. We warn the children: "Don't talk to strangers." We warn ourselves.

This fear of the stranger and foreigner is symptomatic of a culture that is aging, a culture that is almost past its prime. As the poet Goethe once observed, for cultures that are in a stage of development, the new and the foreign are realities to explore with enthusiasm. Such realities are full of promise for a confident culture. However, for cultures in a state of decline, the new and the strange become threatening. The newcomers, the children, the unborn are of least account. We live in a culture more concerned about retirement programs than child care, adequate food, and relief for parents.

Within the Western world, the church is also living on past glories. It is a church in which the new can seem especially threatening—new ways of believing and being. So much is at stake. The future of the church will depend on a ceaseless openness to what is new and unfamiliar.

The Other Face of God

It is a very ancient biblical belief, which the Hebrew prophets constantly recalled, that God is not like us. God is always more than our God, more than we make of him (or her). God is always more than our thought of God. Again and again the prophets reminded the people that God is not an idol, the work of our hands and imaginations. God is always stranger and less familiar than we think. God is the radically New. God is the personification of newness. The Jewish people always set a place at the table for Elijah.

To say we believe in God the creator is to make an act of faith in the constant possibility of newness. Life, as the prophets and Jesus and all spiritual teachers remind us, is not totally within our control. If it is, then it is not life.

Thus, each new child bears the promise of newness and difference. He or she will not simply replicate the patterns of the parents. It is the lifelong challenge of every parent to let his or her child become a different person. This is also the challenge of every marriage, every intimate relationship. The closer we come to someone, the more familiar they become and the more different they seem. I recall a well-known theologian describing his feelings of wonder when he has breakfast with his wife. "I look at her and I realize that I hardly know her at all." This was not a sign that his marriage was in trouble, far from it. It reflected his growing insight into the essential mystery of his wife.

So too refugees burst upon our lives and upon our culture as the newcomers. They bring something quite unexpected into our rather predictable cultural patterns, if we let it be so. Everything depends, I have learned, on whether we expect the unexpected and the new. Once we stop trying to manage the differences of others, we might be taken aback by the fresh gifts that they bring, and a great and new hope.

This is not to say that all differences are delightful. A child or a partner can be disturbingly different, so different that it becomes impossible to imagine sharing a life or a world with them. Some refugees and immigrants are so different that we can easily lose the desire to share a neighborhood or a world in common. However disturbing some differences are, it is probably truer to say that most of us, in this culture, miss the promise of a different way of being.

St. Augustine wrote that God is nearer to me than I am to myself but different enough to make me more than myself. In the pages that follow I want to describe this mystery as I have experienced it—of how we are drawn from a familiar sense of God to an experience of God who is different enough to summon us to become more than ourselves. And the mystery of how the stranger and newcomer, if we stay with them long enough, lead us to a new sense of the nearness of God—to affection and friendship and companionship with God. Living in the shelter of each other, we begin to live in the neighborhood of God.

At Home with God

When did we first
catch sight of You?
When did we know there was
more than meets the eye?
Was it when our mother
lifted us sky high
and we looked down on her
the whole earth beaming back
that it was very good?
Was it when our father
reached out his arms
and waited for us
to stand up and walk

forward, face forward
on our own two feet?
Was it when
she touched us true?
When he saw us
steady and sure?
When
in the time of our lives
did familiarity give birth
to our faith?
And where, or when,
did we first hear
tell of you?
In what intonations
what cadence of language
and longing
in our mother tongue?
Where did we first
feel the length and height of You?
When did the river
become a furrow in our mind?
Where did we learn that you were shelter, storm,
song of the city, lay of the land?
Where? Here. We saw
the familiar face of God.
The God who looks like us
and talks like us—or so we think.
On the border between
here and there

a whole new world is born.
On the border between
the familiar and the strange
something, someone new begins.
Today Christ is born
again along the borderlands
of this world.
In the spaces in between
where cultures meet, border, and salute.

Unfortunately, our culture has arrogantly assumed that most other people in the world would like to be like us or should be like us. Many in that "other world" are now saying poetically and politically that they do not want to be like us, that they want to be different and to be respected as such.

These are the simple and very complex questions that confound our present world politics and our so-called cultural wars. They are the realities we live with every day at Romero House. On a daily basis we welcome strangers from other cultures. More often than not we are summoned to newness in the process.

The Face of Justice

The reflections that follow are occasioned by real encounters between very different people within a particular place. This very real location has given me some insight into some of the "issues" and "problems" of our time. I have come to see that there is a world of difference between a problem and a person with a face and a name. You see things differently, and you solve things differently. You believe differently.

My indebtedness to the insights of the French Jewish philosopher Emmanuel Levinas will be evident throughout this book. Some readers may want to follow my conversation with him in the "Notes on Sources" at the end of this book. Although my thinking diverges from his in one important respect, he has provided me with some helpful ways of articulating what we had already learned at Romero House.

I had been quite active in various issues of peace and justice before I began to live at Romero House. I had traveled extensively, organizing and advocating for "the poor" and "the marginalized." I had written a lot about various issues and concerns. I had worked very hard for very little. I was committed to justice but I had yet to be faced. My heart was still intact. I thought I knew who I was.

Then I met Teresita.

Somehow I was not surprised when the young woman from Guatemala told me her name: "Teresita de Jesús, like in the Bible." She had been holding a tattered brown bible, La Biblia, in her hands since she had first arrived at Romero House. She held on to it for months and read it constantly in the evenings—especially, or so it seemed, in the evenings as I was watching the news on TV.

Teresita and her small son José became my closest neighbors for the next two years, as we shared the kitchen, bathroom, and small living room on the second floor. At first I was a little disconcerted with the small signs of piety that kept appearing about me. On the door of her bedroom she posted a sign "Cristo es Vida." Little prayer cards in Spanish were taped to the mirror in the bathroom and above the kitchen sink. But there were no crucifixes and rosaries. Teresita had become an Evangelical Christian during the years when she lived illegally in the United States, and she did not believe in graven images. Neither did her seven-year-old son. One day he sat looking for a long time at an icon that I had hung in the living room. He turned and looked solemnly at me. "No one has ever seen God's face. Don't you know that?"

Teresita told me she had found Jesus after she arrived in California from Mexico. She had fled from Guatemala after her husband had disappeared, knowing that she was pregnant.

"He was a good man. He was in the army, and they wanted him to do dirty things, and he didn't want to. He told me about the dirty things some of those guys did. And he said they would try to get him. So he told me to get to the border, and he would meet me there. But he never came, and later his cousin called me in California and told me those guys killed him.

"So I had this baby all alone. I know nobody. I sat holding him, and I was so afraid. I didn't know what to do with a baby. I never had a mother. 'What am I going to do with you?' I said to José. That's when I started to go to church. I needed somebody.

"I had a lot of bad things people did to me. When I went to church I began to forgive them. And I felt better. I started to live again."

"Was that when you learned English," I asked.

"Yes, and I got work there. They showed me how to clean, and I volunteered in an old folks place. You know I really like to be with old people and to help them. But after four years they came and said I had to go. I don't know why. The Americans think there is no problem in Guatemala. I don't know why."

The next morning, as she sat tying José's sneakers and getting his lunch ready for school, Teresita resumed our conversation. "You know, I really want to get a job. I don't like to be on welfare. I know this Portuguese guy who's got a cleaning company, and he says I can work for him. It's at night, but I could be back in time to get José ready for school and take him there. Isn't that great?"

Teresita smiled and then hugged José, covering his face with her shimmering hair.

She began to work for minimum wage on a night shift with a cleaning company that had a contract with a large downtown theater. "That's where they have Crazy for You," she said proudly.

"What do you do there?" I asked.

"It's okay. I clean the gum off from under the seats, and I do the washrooms. The boss is okay. He doesn't go after the women." A smile. A giggle.

Every evening Teresita would leave for work around eleven o'clock, returning about half past seven in the morning. José would get up on his own and sit by the front door, waiting for her.

However, after she had been with us for three months, she began to pack her bags. I was extremely distressed when I saw her preparing to leave. She had offered no explanation. Had we offended her? Were we too Catholic for her? Finally, I spoke up. "That doesn't make sense, Teresita. You should stay until we get your immigration status cleared. We would be very sad to see you go."

Teresita put down her suitcase and sat on her bed. "I don't know why I was packing. I never lived anywhere more than three months. I just thought it's three months, and it's time to move on." She sighed. "Nobody ever asked me to stay before."

She stayed.

On her days off, Teresita would clean the kitchen and the bathroom and the living room we shared. I was embarrassed by this, never having had a cleaning lady before. I begged her not to do it.

"I like to work, and besides I've never had a holiday before."

The next weekend I took Teresita and José to a friend's cottage north of the city for a day. As she sat on the porch looking out over the garden as I weeded away, she breathed a big sigh of contentment. "I never had a vacation before." The vacation lasted eight hours, and we returned.

She still insisted on cleaning the living room. "I like to work. Then I don't have to think, and I like to look at your pictures too."

"Oh, which ones?"

"The ones that don't look like a photo. I like paintings like that. They make you think."

"You mean the abstract paintings. But I thought you didn't like to think."

"Oh. You know what I mean. I don't like to think about immigration and about things like that. You know I like that old-fashioned music too—like you play sometimes. It's like what Pavarotti sings. It makes my heart think too."

Because Teresita was such a good cleaner, I had assumed that she knew how to do everything around the house. One day as I was cooking rice, I discovered how little anyone had taught her, how little family life she had had.

"How do you do that? When I cook rice it gets all like glue or burns," Teresita giggled.

"Well, first you wash it in cold water until the water isn't cloudy anymore." I continued with some more tips I had learned from my mother and from some of the other refugee women.

"Oh, I see," Teresita beamed. "I'm going to make it for José tonight. He never liked rice because it tasted so hard and burned."

"I thought every Central American knew how to cook rice and beans."

"Well, you see, I never had a mother. She was an alcoholic and went with men. She sent me to my grandmother, but she never talked to me. My grandfather used to come after me. There was another cousin there, and she was jealous of me. I think because of my curly hair. My grandmother used to beat me, and she would lock me in a room for many days. You know I was so lonely I used to go to a mirror and look at myself and talk to myself. I was so lonely."

Teresita's lips began to quiver and a large tear rolled down the side of her nose.

As the weeks pass I could tell Teresita was getting tired and worried about her refugee process. After she had worked through the night, prepared José's breakfast and lunch and walked him to school, she had only five hours' sleep before he returned home again. She felt terrible that she didn't know how to help him with his homework.

The interns began to spend some time helping José with his homework, and I took on the task of walking José to school. We had some wonderful conversations those mornings.

"You know what I wish most in the world?" he asked.

"What do you wish most in the world?"

"I wish that there is kindness in the world. Can people like us go anywhere in the world?"

"Well, where would you like to go?"

"To the land where Jesus was born."

"I'm a big boy now."

"Yes, you're getting bigger."

"See," he said, pulling up one leg of his jeans, *"the hair on my legs is growing."*

And then he continued, *"Are we going to stay? Can I finish school this year?"*

I had learned that Teresita and José had moved so often that he had never been able to finish a year at school.

I had been talking with Teresita about the refugee process and about the possibility of getting a little money for a lawyer from legal aid. I had done a quick calculation of what I knew she earned and what her expenses might be. I asked if she could contribute $20.00 a month. However, she told me she never had any money left at the end of the month and I believed her. I could see how frugal she was.

"Not even twenty dollars?"

"No. You see, . . . " she hesitated, *"I have another child."*

"Another child! Who? Where?"

"His name is Otavio, and he lives in Mexico. I can show you his picture. They write me a letter every few months about him."

"Who's they?"

"World Vision. Otavio is my adopted son. I send him thirty dollars a month." She brought the tattered picture of him out of her wallet. *"Isn't he cute?"*

"But Teresita, you hardly have enough money to feed José. Why are you doing this?"

"Well, Jesus says that we have to look after those who don't have as much as we do."

So he did.

Teresita initiated only one conversation about her status and that was when I was trying to help her clean the crisper containers in the fridge. Her eyes looked at me over the open door of the fridge, her nose barely touching its rim, her hair slightly astride the jars of mustard and relish below. "If they send me back. . . ." She started to sob and disappeared behind the door.

I stood up and looked over the door. She was kneeling with her forehead touching the floor, her hair spread out like a mop on its surface. "I only have a past. I don't have any future. I never have a tomorrow."

"You've got today," I said putting out my hand, trying to find her face.

"No. I just got a big headache."

As Teresita faced me everyday, I learned that poverty is not simply a social problem to be fixed, not an issue to be addressed.

- Poverty means having a baby alone. Poverty means never having had a mother teach you how to cook rice.
- Poverty means spending your nights cleaning the gum from under the seats that rich people used as they watched a play.
- Poverty means liking the art and music that other people own.
- Poverty means that no one ever asks you to stay.
- Poverty means you can't go anywhere in the world.
- Poverty means that you can't help your child with his homework.
- Poverty means being locked up and lonely and talking to yourself in a mirror.
- Poverty means never having a tomorrow. For the very rich, the future is what you make happen. For middle-class

people, the future is what you plan for, but for the very
poor, the future is just what happens to you.

As I lived with Teresita and José for two years, poverty was
no longer an issue for me, one of my concerns. Poverty had
a face and a name. I understood now how wrong it was to
refer to people as "the poor." They were persons who were, at
this time in their lives, in economic distress. Their immense
complexity and the particular story of their lives could not be
reduced to a social problem called poverty, to a category of
concern or contempt. My desire for justice became focused,
and I knew it would be faithful. It was no longer a hobby, a
part of my life, an issue that I could walk away from when I
wanted to. It would mean giving press conferences to empty
rooms, being crushed by the casual indifference of political
leaders, dismissed as easily as Teresita had been. Justice had
a face, and its name was Teresita.

Such has been my about-face, my conversion. However, I
also believe that this grace is not meant for me alone. I believe
that the blessing bestowed by the stranger reveals the outline
of a spirituality that is crucial for us in this time, in this place
that we call home.

Chapter 1

THE SUMMONS

Only very ancient words describe the depth of what happens when you encounter a stranger. Words like Summons and Commandment, Annunciation and Visitation come almost naturally to mind. They wend their way through the centuries and up through the layers of our selves upon selves. This is how I was summoned by Hidat.

Hidat

It was Palm Sunday, and I was planting tomato seeds in egg cartons on the kitchen table when Zeinab came in with another woman. There were no pleasantries, no polite questions that were customary in any Eritrean encounter. Zeinab was insistent; it could not wait until Easter Monday.

"She is going to be deported in a week," said Zeinab. "I don't understand why she was refused. Her family is one of most prominent members of the opposition party in Eritrea. Her husband disappeared during the Gulf War when the guest workers in Saudi Arabia were forced to drive trucks to the front line. Her sister-in-law is the foreign minister in exile. She and her children would be taken hostage if they are returned to our country."

I looked at the woman next to her. Her head was bowed and her hands rested on the table.

"What is her name?"

"It's Hidat," replied Zeinab.

The woman looked up. Steady and sad.

I was faced.

I had just begun to live with refugees, and I had no idea what I could do to stop this disaster. All of the usual avenues of appeal seemed to have been exhausted. My thoughts scurried about, like a mouse, trying to find a way through the maze of regulations that I had never navigated before.

"I think they make tapes of the hearings," I said. "Try to get a copy of those tapes, and I'll listen to them." To this day I have no idea why this thought came to my mind.

Hidat returned to the house in two days and gave me a manila envelope containing three tapes. She didn't say anything. She didn't know how to speak English. She looked at me. That was all.

It was not until the evening of Holy Thursday that I had time to listen to the tapes. I turned on the cassette machine in the living room and settled in for a long night.

I heard the panel members begin with formalities. I heard their questions and Hidat's faint answers repeated through a translator in English. I began to get sleepy but was jolted back in to consciousness by what seemed to be the sound of a tractor, a motor ticking on and off. I went to the kitchen to see if something was wrong with the fridge. No, the sound was coming from the cassette recorder. No, it wasn't a machine; it was something on the tape. I replayed the section twice. The refugee hearing officer was questioning Hidat. She was floundering. The judges called for a brief recess.

I realized that the sound was that of someone snoring.

A slow fury gathered within me. I called Zeinab even though it was almost midnight. "Call Hidat right away and ask her if her lawyer fell asleep during the hearing and call me back immediately.

Zeinab called back in an hour. "Hidat said the lawyer was sleeping. One of the judges told him to wake up. She didn't think there was anything she could do."

It was a vigil of sorts as I listened to the rest of the tapes as the sun was beginning to rise. Then I prepared the reflections I was to give on one of the stations of the cross during the Good Friday walk through the downtown area.

There was only one reflection left for me to give: "If you want to know what crucifixion means today, then listen to these tapes. Listen as a woman sits alone in a hearing room before two judges as her lawyer, her defender, is snoring away. Listen as she listens to the deafness around her. Listen as she grows silent."

It was eloquent but useless, or so I thought. After the service a young man with his four children came up to the front of the church. "I'm a lawyer. I'd like to help," he said simply.

He did help and was able to get a postponement of the deportation until we had time to listen to the tapes again. With the help of another translator we realized that not only the lawyer was snoring but the translator was completely incompetent. He had mixed up the acronyms of various political parties in Eritrea; he had made a very intelligent woman with immense inner reserves come across as simple and illiterate.

This part of the story has a happy ending. The deportation was stopped. The appeal succeeded. Hidat was given a second hearing and was accepted as a Convention Refugee.

Two years later she was astounded to receive a phone call from her husband. He had spent some time in an Iraqi prison but had been able to escape by promising one of the jailers a ransom fee. All that was left, or so it seemed, was for Hidat to fill out the forms to sponsor him.

That was eighteen years ago. For eighteen years Hidat and I have filled out sponsorship applications, made visits to politicians, filed appeals with the court, given interviews to the press. At one point I went with two other writers and sat in at the office of the Minister of Immigration until we got the promise of some action. Still, the family is separated—by careless politicians, by bureaucratic inefficiency, by a callous cover-up by officials who do not want to admit a mistake.

During these years, Hidat learned English, worked as a hairdresser, raised her three children and finished a nursing degree.

I now know much more than her name. I see her face, the landscape of her particular history. I know she has a wicked sense of humor and is immensely resilient. Her face is the need for justice, the desire for justice, the promise of justice.

The more time I spend with her, the more different she becomes. However, we are not indifferent to each other; we have been through too much together. She is a good neighbor, indeed a good friend. When my mother was dying, Hidat and her sister were there—every day, every night. My relationship with Hidat is a good example of how relationships are transformed over time: we are still different from each other, but we are not so different as to be indifferent to each other.

I was somewhat brave and strong and responsible before I met Hidat. However, I became braver, more tenacious and re-silent, as I responded to the summons that she had presented. I also realized that I was much weaker than I thought, with many fears and unexpected anxieties. So much was at stake.

The Door

It was never my intention to live with refugees. It was not, as they say, part of my game plan. Life, I have learned, is what happens when you are busy planning something else.

I was in between jobs, perhaps in between lives. A friend suggested I take her place as a night manager in a house for refugees. The plan was for me to take her place until a replacement could be found.

"What would be involved?" I asked.

"Just living with them, checking in with them in the evening." The simplicity of the request felt like a summoning. I said yes immediately and moved into the dilapidated old house in the west end.

The plan was that this would be for a month or two. There were other things I had planned to do.

I entered a world of strangers, and we discovered together how to become neighbors. I was blessed to have a remarkable group of women from Eritrea as my guides. Within weeks I discovered that I liked these people, enjoyed having tea with them in the evenings and then dancing in their circle of life.

When it looked as if the religious community who owned the house had to sell it, a group of friends, who had met my new neighbors, gathered together to find a way of continuing this experience. We knew the goodness that was possible when people related to each other as good neighbors rather than as landlords and tenants or social workers and clients. We made conscious decisions to create the conditions in which strangers could become neighbors.

We planned to welcome the stranger. We decided to be open to what is new and different. We decided we would treat each refugee with respect and trust, and this involved some very practical decisions, such as removing all of the locks from the inside of the houses. This was not an easy decision, and it has never become completely automatic over these twenty years. There is always the hesitation, the question, the second thought. You are still anxious when you hear that the captain in the Somali army is arriving with his wife. You wonder about the Sinhalese couple who have just come—haven't they been persecuting the Tamils of Sri Lanka? You have to let go of your fear of losing things. Ultimately, I suppose, you have to let go of your fear of death. You don't ever forget this completely, but you set it aside in the process of responding to the great need and suffering of the people who face you. In twenty years, only one thing has been stolen from my room—a small black and white TV set that was quite useless!

Later you will discover that they have questions about you.

In time, you both change.

In time, you are both transformed in your heart, your mind, and your moral imagination.

In time, you become neighbors.

I know that this experience is not mine alone. It has also

been true many times over, according to church people who have been "faced" by a refugee in great need. They experienced an "about-face," as it were. This is, as Emmanuel Levinas has written, the ethical moment that can define everything that you do and say thereafter. This is the moment when you are summoned, addressed, commanded. This is the time of annunciation and visitation. For many who work with refugees, it is a religious experience.

I would describe the summons by Hidat and others in this way:

> There is a knock at the door
> of the place that structures
> everything that is familiar and safe.
> It is only the sound
> of one hand knocking.
> You can choose not to answer.
> For reasons unclear even to yourself
> you open the door slightly
> and see
> THE EYES and then
> the blur of a face as it looks down
> and then up again.
> It is the face of a stranger,
> the face of a woman.
> You do not know who she is;
> you do not know who you are.
> You could close the door.
> Perhaps she senses this.

The face of a woman with a voice says,
"Please help me."
You could say No.
I am too busy.
I am too tired.
It is too late.
There are other places to go.
I do not know what to do.

You used to know before
you learned how the system can file
people away . . . forever.
You know you are, here and now
the one, the one who must respond:
This YOU *must do. There is no other.*
You have been faced.
The stranger moves forward
and fills the frame of your mind
and slowly comes into focus.
And you become focused.
Your life becomes weighty, consequential, significant.

The Reach of Mercy

This is the core of the ethical experience of Christians who have become involved in working with refugees. These Christians are often rather middle-class people who would not normally associate themselves with peace and justice causes. For many, the encounter with a real person called a refugee evokes feelings of profound compassion that lead to practical forms of kindness. It is within this reach of mercy that the necessity (as well as the near impossibility) of justice begins to emerge.

This is also the core of the experience that binds people to the work of justice and peace for the long haul. As I have spoken to many of these long-haul people in the United States and Canada, I have heard them recall some primary encounter in which they really met and saw a family who was poor, when a small orphan in a medical tent along a war-torn border reached up and grasped their hands and would not let go, when a child who had been abused shrunk into a corner, when they saw the sadness on the faces of the fisherman who pulled up a load of toxic fish.

They are turned inside out.

The crucial thing, of course, is whether we ever really see the persons we have categorized out of our lives. All too often we see and we don't see. We live side by side but not face to face. In many ways our society is structured to prevent us from seeing each other face to face. It is possible to live in a neighborhood composed entirely of people like us, in a gated community or a ghetto of some sort, in a lifestyle enclave of professionals and academics. It is possible to drive to work with people like ourselves and never meet the people we are bundled together with on public transportation.

It also takes a particular attention to hear the summons of the earth that we take so for granted. Barry Lopez's description of the summons of the arctic birds is one of the most eloquent I have ever read:

It was on that evening that I went on a walk for the first time among the tundra birds. They all build their nests on the ground, so their vulnerability is extreme. I gazed down at a single horned lark no bigger than my fist. She stared back as resolute as iron. As I approached, golden plovers abandoned their nests in hysterical ploys, artfully feigning a broken wing to distract me from the woven grass cups that couched their pale, darkly speckled eggs. . . . I took to bowing on these evening walks. I would bow slightly with my hands in my pockets, toward the birds and the evidence of life in their nests—because of their fecundity, unexpected in this remote region, and because of the serene arctic light that came down over the land like breath, like breathing.

It is these moments in which the "issues" of justice or "the environment" dissolve and become refocused so sharply that they are heartfelt. There is no walking away; there is no going back. The way ahead is not clear, but the road has closed behind you. Justice is no longer a sometime thing but a lifelong task.

I have participated in many earnest discussions in church groups about the difference between charity and justice, the works of mercy and the works of justice. The works of mercy are often described as hands-on, one-on-one, direct service of those in need. In contrast, the work for justice involves struggling for systematic change so that there will be less need for charitable activities.

have reflected on my twenty years at Romero House,

I have come to understand that mercy is a dynamic response that begins when one's heart and mind are touched by the need and suffering of another person. We are summoned by mercy. If one begins to act mercifully, as one's compassion deepens and expands, then one is inevitably led to an awareness of the systematic causes of such suffering. At the reach of mercy, one is moved to act with justice. It is this reach of mercy that sustains the passion and commitment to justice. Without mercy, the work for justice becomes critical and calculating. Were it not for the reach of mercy, it would be easy to walk away from the issues and causes of justice.

Without mercy, the categories of concern can also become oppressive, those categories that are only the mirror image of the categories of contempt that are so easily used: the poor, the victims, the abused, the oppressed, the refugees, the marginalized. Even when we use these categories in describing our concern and care, it ends up reducing real people to a category of concern. Of course I often have to use the term "refugees" to describe the situation of the people I live with. However, I try to be careful to describe them as people who once had a place and a country, an identity and work but who are now without all of that. At some point in the future they will no longer be refugees. The category of concern or contempt does not define their whole being.

This is a lesson I learned not only from my neighbors at Romero House but also from one of my students. She had been horribly abused as a child and could have easily described herself in that way. However, she chose to describe herself as someone "who had met evil." It was something that had

front line in Kuwait. He never returned, and because a woman cannot live without her husband in Saudi Arabia, LemLem was forced to leave and came to Canada with her two young sons.

The oldest boy, Robel, was a kind of a child genius who excelled in science. He had joined the science club, and his teachers were already talking about scholarships to the university. The younger boy was totally different and was completely taken up with sports. He set up a hockey net in the backyard to practice. One of the neighbors found him some old equipment, and he was already playing on the school team. Every night the boys worked with one of the interns on their class assignments.

The intern was Darlene O'Leary, and she was the one who really listened to the immense loneliness that LemLem bore. "It doesn't mean when you are a refugee you don't know anything," said LemLem. "We understand. We had a country, home, friends. This makes you. It's easy when you have a home. You can think in your home. You know who you are, and people know who you are. When you don't have a home, you don't have identity. Nobody can understand you. Nobody knows who you are. It's not easy like this. I cry behind doors."

LemLem's application for refugee status was refused because there was very little information available on the situation of the civil war brewing in Eritrea. We decided to submit an application for her to be accepted as an immigrant on humanitarian grounds. This seemed like a good option, as she had taken a hairdressing course, and hairdressers were rather high on the point scale at that time.

A couple of months after the application had been submitted, she was summoned to an interview, and I went with her to the immigration office. We sat behind a thick pane of glass in a small room. A *young officer entered through a door on the other side. He took out his file and clicked his pen.*

"Do you speak English?"

"Yes," she replied. He checked off a box on a form.

"How old are you?"

"Thirty." He checked off another box.

Then he leaned back in his chair. "So what do you think you have to contribute to this country?"

LemLem sat quietly thinking and then responded, "My children."

The officer lurched forward and crossed off the next box.

"That will be all," he said and left the room.

I understood that he had just crossed off her chances to stay in the country. As we left the room, I saw him walking away down the narrow hallway. I went up to him, seething by now.

"She got it right you know. And what would you say if someone asked you what was the most important thing you had to give? Wouldn't you say that your children were the most important gift you had? Shouldn't we say that children are the most important resource this country has?"

He stopped. Blinked. And then turned the corner out of sight.

I had decided not to tell him that one boy could be a great scientist and the other a sport star.

In the end, LemLem and her boys were able to stay, but that is another story. However, that day I had seen someone define what was of value in the country. This officer clearly did not think children were of great value. He probably thought of them as another expense for the government. Who defines who is of value and why? What the narrow little categories of the immigration department had missed was the most important gift that LemLem and her boys brought with them. They brought a modest hope in the country, the hope that we could be a good country, a just country.

Chapter 2

THE EMPIRE OF THE SELF

The stranger, the newcomer, often comes as a shock to your sense of yourself. The child doesn't care about your wardrobe or your most recent promotion. He just wants to be fed and now. The stranger doesn't understand a word of your beautiful English. She just needs a place to sleep and now. Someone else is taking a measure of your life.

The size and shape of your life are seen from a different perspective. The life you have taken for granted now seems rather strange. I saw my life rather differently after I had meet Gugan, Yuri, and Deequa. The insurance executive from Sri Lanka and the economist from Azerbaijan showed me how thoroughly middle-class and professional my life had become. The woman from Somalia revealed how subtly self-centered we can become because of where we live.

Gugan

It was imperceptible at first, the slight additions in our mailbox. A catalogue for office equipment one day, a flyer for cellular phones the next day, and then a brochure for VCRs. It was nothing I had ordered and everything we couldn't afford at Romero House. Junk mail, I thought, and ditched it into the wastepaper basket without bothering to read it further.

The mail continued. Day by day, packets arrived from travel agencies, from government information offices, garden clubs, book and music companies. Coupon books, postcards from companies, directories of services. "Thank you for inquiring," "In response to your request." Pitch and ditch.

Then came the morning when I had to make two trips from the mailbox to my desk. It took me twenty minutes to find the two or three letters that seemed to relate to Romero House business. I marched out to the mailbox and taped my protest against consumerism: NO JUNK MAIL PLEASE.

The volume of mail decreased dramatically during the following days. I was relishing my small victory in the cosmic war against junk when Gugan appeared at the door of the office. "Has my mail arrived?" he asked expectantly.

"No, I didn't see any for you Gugan. Were you expecting an important letter?"

He slumped in the chair by my desk. He crumpled in front of me. "It was just some catalogues I had sent for. I saw the advertisements in the paper, and I, thought, well, I thought it would be nice to get some mail even if I can't buy anything. I don't get much mail now. I used to get a lot of mail every day in my office."

Gugan had told me that he had been a senior vice president of an insurance company in Sri Lanka.. With a sigh of contrition I realized that I had thrown some of the few remaining props for whatever was left of his identity.

"I'm sorry Gugan, I didn't realize the catalogues were addressed to you. I should have looked more carefully."

"What you need is a good executive secretary, like the one I used to have," he smiled modestly.

"Well," I said, "why don't you take responsibility for improving the delivery of mail to everyone in the houses? I'm sure you would be much more efficient."

"I would be delighted. It's what you call an entry-level position. He straightened up and walked out like someone you would call a businessman.

Gugan had made me aware of how one's economic class affected one's identity in the most subtle ways. Although I was not wealthy in the way that Gugan had once been, I realized that most of the people I associate with get a lot of mail, a lot of e-mails. This mail confers a sense of importance on us. The mail makes the man, or woman. I suspect being well positioned within the knowledge industries makes us think that people who don't get a lot of mail aren't that important.

Yuri

An economist from Azerbaijan walked around with his briefcase all the time. He took it with him to English class; he kept it by his side as he was watching TV in the common room. He also looked like a businessman. He lived in the same house as me.

In the middle of one night the house phone began to ring, and I got up to answer it. The connection was poor, but I was able to understand that the phone call was for Yuri. I went upstairs and knocked on his door. As he opened the door I could see that the briefcase was underneath the pillow on his bed.

The next morning I met Yuri on the stairs and decided to ask the question that I had been asking myself for weeks. "Yuri, I can see the briefcase is important for you. If you have something really important in it you can put it in our safe in the office."

I tried to communicate this question with careful gestures. He understood.

"Nothing there," he said. "Nothing. Only me."

I wondered who I would be without my briefcase or my knapsack? Who would my friends be without their laptop case? Who would we be without our place in the world? Who would we be outside of our network of purpose?

Deequa

Deequa lived on the same floor as the office because she found it difficult to go up and down the stairs.

When she arrived at our house, in her gorgeous long Somali dress, we could see immediately that she had a limp, and so we tried to make things as accessible as possible for her, arranging for Wheel-Trans to take her to English classes. Little by little we were able to communicate through more than smiles and chuckles.

One Saturday evening, Deequa finally confided in Winkie, a nurse who is a friend of Romero House. "I need a new leg," she said.

Slowly pulling up her dress, Deequa revealed the stick that was attached to the rough wooden stump just above where her knee had once been. Winkie examined the festering sores around the piece of old wood and then called in one of the Somali women to translate.

As the story slowly came out, Deequa told them of the day the house she had been living in had been bombed. Her leg had been torn to shreds, and she was filled with pieces of the bomb. Winkie explained that we called this shrapnel. With great delicacy, Winkie examined the rest of Deequa's body and saw that there were pieces of shrapnel in her abdomen and chest and in her arms. She had been in continuous pain, but all that was veiled behind her smile.

Winkie referred Deequa to a doctor, and every few weeks one of the interns would drive Deequa to get a few more pieces of shrapnel removed.

The process of getting a new leg was to prove more of a challenge. Deequa was taken to a hospital where she was carefully, meticulously, measured for a better prosthesis by some very fine medical technicians. In the meantime, she was given a thick metal pole to which a large shoe was attached.

At last the much awaited day arrived, and Peter, one of the interns, drove Deequa to the hospital to be fitted with the new leg. We had planned a big party and had posted announcements in all of the Romero houses for the "Take Back the Leg" party.

As they were driving home from the hospital Peter ventured to ask, "Well how does it feel, Deequa?"

"Good," she replied, and then she lifted her dress modestly to mid-calf level.

"They didn't have my color," she laughed.

Peter looked down and saw a very white leg. He didn't know what to say.

I didn't know what to say when they returned, and Deequa showed me her whiter than white leg.

"They" didn't have her color. They thought they had constructed a very fine leg, a far better leg than the wooden stump she had hauled along from Somalia. They probably thought she should be grateful, and she was. But they didn't think that the color mattered. They didn't even think to try to stain the leg darker. Who wouldn't want a white leg? White was normal. White was the best. I realized that the color of her leg was Imperial White.

The newcomer, the stranger, brings a new insight into the world that we take for granted. Those of us who live in North America tend to think that where we live is reality and how we live is normal. It is not that we are morally or spiritually obtuse. It is simply a fact that it is very difficult to "see" our own culture. Like fish in the water, we do not know the culture in which we live and move and have our being.

Gugan, Yuri, and Deequa had enabled me to see my own context through another set of eyes. I saw that I was living in the Center of the World. I saw that this made all the difference in the world.

America Is the Center of the World

America is now the Center of the World. Since the fall of the Soviet Union, and indeed before 1991, the United States has been the predominant economic, political, and military power in the world. It is also the homeland of a universally popular culture. All eyes are on America, for as America goes, so goes the world.

Canada, as the nearest and largest quasi-colony of the

American empire, also shares the sense of living close to the center of the world. This is not just a geographic fact; it is also a matter of social and political consciousness.

Most people would agree, for the moment, that the United States is the number one power in the world today. What is decided in the White House, in Congress, on Wall Street, in the corporate boardrooms of America influences the rest of the world greatly. Few would dispute that this is a political, economic, and military fact. However, we need to reflect more deeply on how this fact affects our personal and spiritual lives.

My neighbors, the refugees at Romero House, have many stories to tell about how their lives were directly or indirectly affected by political and military decisions made in the center of the world. We are still receiving refugees whose lives were cast up into the winds of history by the first Gulf War in 1990. Many Eritreans and Somalis who were living in Saudi Arabia at the time of the outbreak of the war were forced to drive vehicles to the front. Many never returned; they were killed or put in Iraqi prisons for years. Their wives and children were forced to leave Saudi Arabia to begin a journey of years in search of safety.

The war was over rather quickly for the powerful ones living in the center of the world. However, the war continues on in thousands of lives, in other countries, in refugee camps along the borders of this world.

Most refugees can tell you where the center of the world is: they fear this place, and they flee to it for safety. They know that the American empire rules the world.

Almost twenty years ago, I began to suggest that we were living in the time of the American empire. At that time, even socially aware Americans were reluctant to admit that this was an accurate description of their country. Most Americans are so shaped by the founding stories of the republic that they find it difficult to think of themselves as the rulers of empire. The early struggle for independence from the British empire has so shaped the imagination of a nation that it makes it more difficult to see that the once small colony has now become an empire.

For many years I had the privilege of team teaching a variety of courses with Sr. Margaret Brennan IHM. She was an American who, for twenty years, had graced Regis College in Toronto with her wisdom. We would inevitably discuss the realities of empire with our students. On a few occasions she came into the classroom waving an American flag! Our perspective on the empire was rather different and for good reasons. It seemed obvious to me that we in Canada had the rather frequent experience of having our lives directed by decisions in head offices elsewhere—in Paris, London, and now in New York and Washington. One of our former prime ministers had said that living next to the United States was "like sleeping with an elephant." We have to know what is going on in America because we are affected by every twist and turn of what happens there. The word "empire" forced me to think about the difficult consequences of living in a colony of empire, about the tendency to think that THERE always seems so much more important than HERE. (And it usually is more important).

For Margaret, trying to think about her country as an empire was much more challenging. She had a deep and loyal sense of the founding ethos of the republic, a republic that revolted against the oppressive reach of the British empire, a republic that set a limit on political and religious forms of imperialism. Margaret was very aware of injustices that her country had perpetuated in other parts of the world (Vietnam, Central America) but she just did not feel comfortable with the thought of living in the heart of empire.

That was then and this is now. George Bush became the imperial president, a fact celebrated by some and criticized by others. Both Margaret and I are discovering what it means to think along the border called the forty-ninth parallel.

It is a confusing political situation for those at the center of the empire and those on its periphery: on the one hand, there is the rhetoric of the republic—the ideals of liberty and justice for all—and on the other hand, there are the realities of military and economic power. And Americans have ways of distancing themselves from the imperial havoc that is sometimes wreaked on other parts of the world: the "government" is guilty and responsible for these bad deeds; the government is off waging wars in far-off places, and "the people" are as innocent as apple pie; "the people" are the most enthusiastic volunteers in the world and attend little league games in small towns on Sunday afternoon. Nevertheless, as Reinhold Niebuhr wisely observed, the tragedy of being a great political power is that it is impossible to be great and to be good at the same time.

We see and we do not see. We hear and we do not hear.

I now see that the weight of empire is borne not only by those outside of North America. Those of us who have grown accustomed to living in this particular place, at this particular time in history, have also been profoundly affected by this reality. Living in the Center of the World has also shaped our personal identity. It has generated some very particular psychologies and spiritualities.

The Imperial Self

The Imperial Self is the phrase I would use to describe the psychological correlative of the social reality of living in the Center of the World. To put it simply, it is easier to be self-centered when you live in the Center of the World; it is easier to think of the rest of the world as revolving around your needs and desires when you live in a place that the rest of the world is watching.

Self-centeredness is probably part of the human condition. It is the tendency that all the wise and ancient spiritual masters counseled against. Yet, it takes on a particular energy and different forms of temptation in this context.

The arrogant and violent forms of self-centeredness are probably obvious to most North Americans who are earnestly seeking a more spiritual way of life. Yet, the temptation to self-centeredness exists even for those who are sincerely repelled by the patterns of domination through violence in their culture.

There are those who are painfully aware that their self is the source of many problems, not only for themselves but also for

others. They are earnestly working on their selves in a search
for healing that will help their partners, their children, their
co-workers. The assumption is that the self is the source of
all kinds of personal problems, and the self is the source of
possible solutions.

Let us consider the profound way in which this imperial
attitude affects our relationships with other people—those
near and dear to us and those who are different and from
afar. An imperial spirituality will tend to assume that my attitude to other people is shaped by my needs and desires, by
my generosity or self-interest. I care for others because I am a
caring person. I help others because I am a generous person,
because I come from a generous family or I have grown up
in a generous community. In other words, my response to
others is a function of who I am. Thus, some spiritualities of
service will emphasize the importance of discovering one's
true self, of becoming a good Christian, before we begin to
serve others.

It all depends on me. Or it all depends on my God.

The spiritual shape of imperialism appears.

There are also socially engaged persons who still believe
that it is America's manifest destiny to bring political and
economic blessings to the world. Others have more the modest
goal of making America once more a City on a Hill, a good
example for the rest of the world. Even more critical persons,
who no longer have such illusions, still see America as the
source of all the problems in the world. In the end, they say,
America is responsible for all economic, environmental, and
political disasters in the world. One way or another, these

political activists are all seeing America as the center of the world and their actions of ultimate and world importance.

The burdens of the imperial self are immense. We are responsible for all the good and all the bad in the world. Much depends upon us.

- To live in the center of the world is to see the self as the source of much that is good and evil in the world.
- To live in the center of the world is to assume that we can and should change the world.
- To live in the center of the world is to be constantly disappointed when things don't get better.
- To live in the center of the world is to assume that our problems are the most important in the world.
- To live in the center of the world is to assume that we must have our act together before we can help others.
- To live in the center of the world is to assume that we have the capacity and the resources to solve our problems.
- To live in the church in North America is to assume that our critique of the church is the most important, that our problems are the most significant problems in the universal church.
- To live in the center of the world is to assume that we are responsible for what happens in other parts of the world.

And finally, how does living in the Center of the World influence our image of God? It would probably shape an imperial image of God, the image of a God who is or should be in control of all things. It would probably make us tend to imagine that our God is much more important and significant than the God or gods of all other religions. It would probably lead us to believe that our God is more loving, more merciful, and more just than any other God.

Will the renewed desire for spirituality lead to a deeper self-centeredness or to a more profound sense of connectedness with others? The temptation to become self-centered is difficult to resist—not because we are unusually weak or spiritually obtuse. No, the temptation is so strong because of the overwhelming reality of the culture that we live in. The culture of imperialism is in the very air that we breathe, infecting even our most courageous social efforts and our sincerest desires to live more spiritually.

Conversion to the True Self

We are in need of a foundational spiritual conversion. How can we be saved from ourselves? Fortunately, we have at least one spiritual guide who understood the depth of the spiritual challenge posed by the culture that we live in. Thomas Merton articulated the spiritual journey as the way out of the false self toward the true self. As he described it, the false self is indeed the self that sees itself as the center of the world. The false self, or the ego, is the self that we try to manufacture, the self that is under construction and under control. This false self attempts to place all other people, and even God, under control. This is the self that sees other people as objects of interest, objects of contempt or concern. Everything and everyone is subservient to this self: the rest of the world, other people, even God.

"People who know nothing of God and whose lives are centered on themselves, imagine that they can only find themselves by asserting their own desires and ambitions and appetites in a struggle with the rest of the world."

The true self, on the other hand, is the self that is given, that is beyond our control. It is the mysterious ground of our life that we can never lay hold of. This true self, according to Merton, moves us beyond ourselves to deep communion with the true selves of others. The more we transcend ourselves truly, the closer we come to others and to God.

Merton stands as the representative of one of the most important strands of spirituality in North America today: the search for a deep and true subjectivity. The goal of this search is to live an authentic subjectivity, to live as a self that transcends itself.

Becoming Good

What I am describing in this book is another strand of spirituality that promises its own way of liberation. The false self is the imperial self. However, it can be thrown off center by the summons of the other, the stranger, and the newcomer. The newcomer and the stranger are the ones who break through our silly attempts to control the world. We are disoriented and reoriented when we are faced by them. This is the blessing. It is the stranger who summons us to become our true selves. The newcomer and the stranger need us to be good, to be true, to be responsible.

I recall listening to the conversation between a young Mexican boy and one of our neighbors who had volunteered to teach him English. She was trying to encourage him and said earnestly, "Let's go, Alberto. You can be number one if you just work a little harder." He was silent for a while and then said simply, "I'd like to be number five." He did not want to be great, but he did want to be good, good enough.

There is a whole strand of Western ethical thought that argues that we must be good before we can do good. In some contemporary spiritualities this is articulated as the importance of being ourselves before we can be for others. We must know Jesus before we can follow him.

However, it is also possible that we become good in the process of doing good. We become who we truly are as we respond to the summons of the other; we come to know Jesus as we follow him. It is in responding to the annunciations and visitations of the strangers that our lives become weighty, consequential, significant.

We respond to the call of another not because we are good but because the command of the other activates the goodness between us. The stories in this book are testimonies of how I became myself in responding to the summons of those who knocked at my door. They knocked at the door of my known world, the rather predictable world of me and the God who had become all too familiar. It was a blessed disorientation.

In the later chapters of this book I want to explore how we can become Christians in responding to the summons of the newcomers and strangers.

The Shock of Limitation

There is another characteristic of the imperial culture affects us spiritually. Just as an imperial culture is inherently expansionary, so too we are inclined to think of our very selves as almost naturally expansive. Not to grow is to die. We are now at a critical point in the life cycle of this particular empire of America. Whereas once we took growth of any kind for granted, now it is somewhat in doubt. This is most evident in the area of the economy that has been in a recession for some time. The United States is the largest debtor nation in the world, and it is indebted largely to one of the new emerging centers of the world: China. Recent G-20 meetings have showcased the fact that there are now several economic centers of the world: in addition to China, there is India, Russia, the European Union, Brazil.

America still remains the most significant military power in the world, but the economic center of power is slowly but surely shifting. It is a moment of great political significance. However, it is of immense spiritual importance as well.

It matters that this center is not holding. It matters that this empire may have entered the first phase of its decline. Economically and politically we are being thrown off center.

For many this is a profoundly disorienting experience. Old assumptions and certitudes seem to have lost their power. Economically and politically we are losing control of the world. It matters that this empire in which we find our identity, meaning, and purpose is no longer progressing and developing. Very few American parents are sure that their children will be better off. This is an immense social shock. Generations of people were willing to work hard, to sacrifice to ensure that their children would be better off. Many people studied long and hard so they could have a better life. Millions of people immigrated to Canada and the United States in search of prosperity.

The belief in the myth of progress is experienced on the ground and in daily life as the simple conviction that tomorrow will be better than today—if we just work hard enough and think smart enough. This optimism is now wavering. It is a spiritual shock of immense proportions.

For many Americans their faith had become subtly intertwined with the positive and confident attitude of empire. Great missionary and evangelical projects, great movements of social justice were grounded in the optimistic belief that the world could be changed—if we just worked hard enough and thought smart enough. Everyone could grow personally and succeed if they tried. If someone was poor or unsuccessful, it was simply because he or she had not worked hard enough or wasn't smart enough.

In his last analysis of the state of mind in America, the perceptive social commentator Tony Judt concluded that "Ill Fares the Land."

We have entered an age of fear. Insecurity is once again an active ingredient of political life in Western democracies. Insecurity born of terrorism, of course; but also, and more insidiously, fear of the uncontrollable speed of change, fear of the loss of employment, fear of losing ground to others in an increasingly unequal distribution of resources, fear of losing control of the circumstances and routines of our daily life. And, perhaps above all, fear that it is not just *we* who can no longer shape our lives but that those in authority have also lost control, to forces beyond their reach.

The faith of many, in their country, in themselves, is being deeply shaken. Many are turning to religion to regain some sense of control. I remember giving a talk in Texas in which I suggested that the power of God was not a controlling power but rather the power to create something or someone new. After the talk a man came up to me and said, "Honey, I just want you to know that my God is in charge." His was the Imperial God. Is it any wonder that our need to control, to have someone in control, increases as our established world seems increasingly out of control?

Are We Rome?

There is now a public debate about whether America is the new Rome. A number of contemporary thinkers are now analyzing the situation of America today through the lens of history. Is America like Rome? Is it in a process of decline? Has it fallen or will it fall?

According to Yale historian Paul Kennedy there is a kind of historical arc to all empires: they usually begin as small political units such as republics and then gradually expand. The colonies are subdued to provide goods and services for the political center. This is the process of empire building: Rome, Spain, England, and now the United States. To keep the colonies under control, a permanent and large military apparatus is developed. There is a cultural optimism in such a process. However, at some point the economic base of the empire is unable to support this expanding military apparatus and the empire begins a process of decline, which may be rather fast or extremely slow. Rome, for example did not decline in a day but over a period of centuries. The "fall" of Rome in 410 A.D. was actually a short-lived intrusion that destroyed part of the city, but not all. The shock of 410 A.D. was that Rome, the center of the then known world, had been attacked. Rome, which had been considered eternal, was revealed as vulnerable.

By 410 A.D. Christianity had become the religion of empire, and so the question for theologians was what the collapse of this state meant for the religion of Christianity. If Rome had become the vehicle for the spreading of Christianity, would this mean a crisis of faith? Or if Rome was the anti-Christ, was this an event that could and should be celebrated? The struggle for the early Christians was to find true hope when cultural optimism had failed.

In his monumental book, *The City of God*, Augustine struggled with the spiritual implications of the fall of Rome. He concluded that Rome was neither a good empire nor an evil empire. It was a mix of both good and evil, just as good and evil are mixed within each person. Thus, he said that Christians could work for the good of "the City" but could never give complete allegiance to any political entity.

Augustine described the two cities: the City of God and the City of Man, Jerusalem and Babylon, as mixed within human history. The citizens of these two cities were defined by the desire of their hearts, those who desire good and those who desired evil. This citizenship would only be revealed at the end of time. In short, this was a time of disorientation for the Christians who lived within the Roman Empire. Those who had identified their faith with the empire were thrown off center. Augustine encouraged them to center their lives on the City of God, on the love of God and neighbor. The City of God was experienced here on earth in the small communities of like-spirited people who shared the same love of God and neighbor. These were the beloved communities.

In the time of the decline of Rome, Augustine did not counsel great world-shaping projects. He did not advise great expansionary visions of bigger and better forms of Christianity. Instead, he wrote about small local communities united by a common and humble spirit of service. The early forms of monasticism reflected this small and simple form of Christianity after empire.

This modest form of Christianity seems to be suggested in a contemporary form in Don DeLillo's novel *Underworld*. The book is a brilliant description of the Cold War period and how it shaped the consciousness of America. The illustration on the cover of the book shows an old parish church situated against the backdrop of the twin towers, then symbols of economic power. Eerily enough, a plane seems to be flying into the towers, although the book was written before 9/11. The old church is the home base for Franciscan friars who go into the underground world of the subways and graffiti artists to deliver food to the hungry.

Listen to the Stranger

The spiritual challenge of this time and place is to find the true center, the new center of our lives. It means allowing our lives to be thrown off center and embracing the disorientation that this implies.

The stranger can become the guide in times such as these. The stranger can summon us to leave behind our imperial selves, our imperial lives.

However, the promise that the newcomer and the stranger offer is not usually recognized in our culture. More often than not they are treated as at least a problem and usually as a threat, a danger. Generally speaking, this is not because we are mean and prejudiced people, but it does indicate the kind of social attitudes that we have interiorized, attitudes that flourish as a culture begins to enter a process of decline. The need for enemies becomes greater as the social vision that holds an empire together begins to wane. The enemy becomes the glue that holds a society together. During the long Cold War period, America gradually became more defined by what it was against than whom or what it was for. It defined itself by being against communism more than by being for democracy.

When this great enemy fell, there was a new need for enemies, and a small succession of enemies filled the bill for a while. However, with the shocking event of 9/11 a new and great and all-pervasive enemy emerged: the terrorist.

We divided the world into friends who are like us and enemies who are not like us. The stranger became the enemy.

This is our contemporary form of the Manichean dualism that Augustine so criticized. He thought it was heresy to divide the world into good empires and evil empires, between the good like us and the evil who are not like us. Contemporary writers as diverse as Solzhenitsyn and John Le Carré have reworded this caution and stated that the line between good and evil goes through the heart of each one of us. It is not out there; it is in here, in each one of us.

Those who are seeking to live their faith in the context of America in the post-9/11 reality need to think long and hard about their underlying theological assumptions about the way the world is, about the way people are. Just as it is tempting to cast the refugee as either a morally superior being or a socially inferior type, it is also tempting to divide the world between the unjust and the just.

Our challenge is to remain life-size in a time diminished by terror.

Chapter 3

THE CONCENTRATED LIFE

Clara

It was several years before I could really talk with Clara. My Spanish was rather basic, and her English was nonexistent. However, we liked each other immediately and communicated in our own way. We laughed a lot together. I had never met anyone who was so much fun . . . and so focused.

She had worked hard ever since she was a teenager and eventually became the owner of a haute couture fashion store in a large city in Colombia. Clara was well known there as the designer of elegant dresses that were always in demand. Her business employed almost a hundred people and was highly profitable. However, in her own opinion the most important fact about her life was that she had two sons.

This storybook world was shattered when she received a threat from the ultra-leftist group FARC–either you give us all your profits every month or you die. Clara knew that the FARC demands would never be satisfied and would escalate over time. Given the realities of Colombia, there was no other choice: she packed a bag, walked out of her business, and said good-bye to her sons. The loss of her business meant nothing to her, but the separation from her sons was heartbreaking. She cried for months but kept on moving.

After a long journey through Mexico and some time in the United States, she eventually made it to the Canadian border and claimed refugee status. She immediately realized how restricted her options were because she did not know English. She went to class every day, although she never progressed beyond the first level. Undaunted, she set about starting a cleaning business with two other women. They called themselves "Los Tres Primeras" and began to expand their work with several houses in the neighborhood. On the side, she developed a special kind of cooking utensil that would facilitate the production of Colombian arepas. These arepas soon became a feature at all our Romero House parties.

Every month Clara sent money back to Colombia to the relatives who were looking after her sons. They were on her mind, but she was never morose. She was kind and generous to everyone she met and became my good neighbor, as we lived in the same house.

I have a vivid memory of the fall when we were awaiting the arrival of a new intern at our house. The week before his arrival, Clara asked me to write out a sentence to welcome him. She said the sentence over and over for days. When the young guy finally arrived, a little dazed from his long flight, Clara was waiting for him at the front door: "My name is Clara. Pleeezed to meet you." She beamed with delight and repeated the sentence several times. "Yeah, me too," the young man replied. That was all she could say, but it was more than enough. He knew he was welcome.

Eventually Clara had a refugee hearing and was accepted. The next day she began to fill out the forms to sponsor her sons. She had already saved enough money from her various businesses to pay for the application fees. Normally, the process takes about a year and a half, but after three years the sons still had not arrived.

She marched into my office with an order: "I want my sons. Now." I began phoning the embassy in Bogotá. Initially, I was quite polite, but as the runaround continued, I became aggressive, pushy, as demanding as Clara. "I want those boys here. Now."

Soon after this close encounter with bureaucratic incompetence, Clara and I spent a week together at the Romero House summer camp. She was lighthearted and expectant, sure that her sons would be here soon. At one of the social gatherings that week she did a fabulous skit as the backup to the famous singer Celia Cruz.

After we returned from camp, Clara had sudden and severe pains in her abdomen. After some medical tests, the doctor told her that she had inoperable cancer and had very little time to live. "I want my sons. Now."

I made some more calls to Bogotá. The embassy official wanted a letter from the doctor. He got it. Then he e-mailed back to ask for another letter so he could be sure that she was not just sick but dying. I yelled over the phone. "She has the right to sponsor her children dead or alive!" Another official asked for a copy of her x-ray so he could be sure she was sick or dying.

Clara was taken to the hospital and was slipping in and out of consciousness. The doctor said she would die that night. I phoned the embassy again, pleading. The officer said they had just issued the visa; the sons said it would take another two days to get the ticket. They had not really registered how precarious her situation was. They couldn't believe that she was really dying.

Clara held on through the night . . . and another night. Finally, the boys arrived at the airport where someone picked them up and *took them directly to the hospital. She was unconscious but still alive. Her sons knelt by her bed and tried to talk with her. I believe she heard them. An hour later she was dead.*

Clara's comfortable world in Colombia had collapsed, but her life had remained focused. All of the desperate hours she had spent scrubbing and dusting and mixing and flipping had a purpose—to be with her sons again. Even death could not deflect her from this point of her being.

Osman

I saw this intense focus again in the person of Osman Omar.

Osman Omar was another Eritrean who showed up in the kitchen of Romero House. He came on his own. He pulled up a chair and sat down beside the table where I was working on an article. A small and wiry man, he was agitated and anxious. He spoke English well, and so he proceeded to speak even before I offered him tea.

"I am a well-known journalist in Eritrea. I edited a newspaper that was very critical of the present government. I was refused by the refugee board because they don't understand that a civil war is taking place in our country. I am going to be deported. I have a wife and ten children. You must help me."

I didn't know what to say. "You must help me," he insisted. He looked at me in a terrified way and wound his hands together and then rested his head upon them.

I put my head in my hands. "OK."

This was really the beginning of the sanctuary movement in central Canada. It would absorb much of the next twenty years of my life. Everything I had learned and everyone that I knew would be brought to bear on the fate of fourteen Eritrean families who were in the same situation as Osman Omar. In the process I discovered who I was—better than I thought, worse than I knew.

Brother John Masterson, another member of the sanctuary movement, found a hiding place for this family in one of the Jesuit houses. I would go out and give talks to raise money, and he would bring the money to the family. After almost a year we had gained a tentative agreement from the government that they would not be deported.

However, it would take years before the family was finally accepted into the country. Although the family had been accepted by the Minister of Immigration, the officials handling "the file" insisted that Osman have a job and that he pass a medical. This presented a hurdle that seemed almost impossible to overcome as Osman was already partially blind.

Years passed, and even though the oldest children were working and supporting the family, it did not matter to the officials who were still insisting that Osman himself had to work. Without the final papers, the oldest children could not go to university. They did not complain, but their father felt their lives were wasting away.

Osman decided to get a job, any job, so the family would have a better chance of regularizing its status. His efforts were further frustrated when a routine eye operation was botched, and he was left legally blind.

Desperate but still determined, he took a job that hardly anyone would want. He went out with a road crew and held signs for traffic he could barely see. I went out to visit him on a cold winter day. He was standing in the middle of the road, his eyes barely visible in the scarf he had wound about his head. Although he couldn't see the cars coming from either direction, he simply turned the stop sign to go when the other workers yelled at him. "He's going to get killed out here," I thought.

However, he didn't die on the road. He got cancer and died very suddenly. Osman Omar never got any official status in the country. Eventually, his children received the papers he had struggled so bravely to secure.

The writer who had once written courageous editorials never seemed braver than when he stood in the middle of the road with the snow swirling about him, blind to everything except the feeling of intense cold. Like most refugees, he had been left with only bits and pieces of his former life. He had arrived with a collection of fragments of his past in a suitcase.

Osman Omar spent years waiting and waiting. Once upon a time he had been very busy. He too had a briefcase and got a lot of mail. Like many refugees, he had lost the framework of meaning that once held his life together, a cause, a political party, a hope for change that inspired many to sacrifice their lives. They have been forced to abandon that dream. Writers like Osman Omar, who once knew who they were in the cadence of their language, were compelled to leave the cultural matrix in which they lived and moved and had their being.

More often than not, it is the children who get them up out of bed in the morning. They feed their children even when they have lost their appetite. They walk their children many blocks to school and then return home again. In another time and place, their chauffeur had driven the children to school. The day is measured out by the needs of the children, their school, their meals. In the afternoon, one of the parents will go to the food bank.

However, there are hazards in making children the only focus of their parents' lives. The children are burdened with great expectations that they cannot always fulfill.

The refugees who survive the upheaval are the ones who seem to have found something else that demands great concentration: the learning of a language, the challenge of taking a car engine apart and putting it together again, the perfection of the guitar. These activities help them refocus a life that has fallen into fragments.

Cultural Fragmentation

The upheavals that define a refugee are not totally different from the sense of upheaval experienced by many North Americans. We are living in a culture and in a time where the larger frameworks of meaning no longer hold our lives together. The large narratives that helped us situate our lives are no longer persuasive. We are losing not only a religious framework of meaning but also the secular framework of meaning that has shaped our culture for more than two hundred years. We are, as it were, chapters in search of a book.

In the past, the underlying narrative structure of our lives was supplied by our culture, by our country, or by religion, sometimes even by sports. The modern myth of progress carried our lives forward by the sheer force of its optimism ever since the founding of America. This is the myth that undergirds the myths of empire. It is an essentially expansionary view of life: bigger, stronger, better. In economic terms, the system grows or dies. Consumerism is fueled by this craving for expansion—more and more. In politics, if the empire is not expanding, it is being defeated. In spiritual and personal terms, this leads to unquestioned assumptions about the importance of personal growth and development: either you grow or you die.

These lifelines still exist, but they no longer seem strong enough to pull us out of our culture of consumerism, with its attendant fragmentation and clutter. The events of the twentieth century, simultaneously barbaric and eminently modern, have raised doubts about the myth of progress in a way that no philosophical critique could do. The founding ideals of the republic are becoming lost in the imperatives of empire. To the extent that the mainline religions tied their message to the dominant myths of culture, their voices too have become uncertain and lost.

Remnants of Religion

Within various church communities, we find ourselves similarly fragmented. Only a few Catholics, for example, would pretend that we are still guided by a single and integrated vision of life and the world. We are sustained by fragments of a tradition, beautiful fragments, true fragments. However, there often seems to be no whole greater than these parts. Most Catholics return to Mass on Christmas Eve and rejoice in the sense of mystery that is communicated through the sacraments. But they no longer sense the whole world as breathing with some mysterious significance. The day after Christmas, McDonald's is McDonald's; a hamburger is a hamburger, and the more the better. Religion is for certain times and places, here and there, more or less—and always in moderation.

In the past, generations of people could situate their small lives within a larger story of meaning. A family could find the whole focus of meaning in building the great cathedral of Chartres. Their whole lifetime was invested in rolling a stone up the hill, in creating a stained-glass window. In the Western world today, very few people have the sense that they are part of building a great cathedral.

So too within our sociopolitical experience it is difficult to see how the sacrifice of so many makes sense. It did make sense for the noblest generation to give their lives in the fight against Nazism. However, the fight against the Taliban is not against a great enemy but a nimble one. Ever since the Vietnam War, the noble struggle seems harder to find.

We are losing sight of secular and religious visions that have shaped our lives and given us a sense of meaning and purpose. These were the visions that helped us know our place and purpose in life, the point of living and dying.

We are left with fragments of meaning, religious fragments, political fragments, which are not meaningless but which do not serve to situate our lives and make them whole. There are many bits and pieces to our lives, but they do not fit together; we are not whole. Our crucial spiritual challenge is how to focus our lives in meaningful ways in the absence of compelling narratives of meaning.

We are people who are living in what I have called "episodes of meaning." We cannot find the story line, the narrative structure that strings together all the various episodes of our lives. There seems to be no beginning, no definitive turning point or end, no conclusion.

A culture that lives on episodic meanings is one in which it becomes ever more difficult to lead consequential lives. If there is no connection between the episodes of our lives, why should it matter what we do and how we live? Episodes of meaning do not add up to direction or purpose, and they may even intensify our sense of meaninglessness and powerlessness. For Clara, for Osman, for my North American friends, is there any thread of meaning, any sense of direction and purpose that flows through our days and holds them together?

Clutter and Junk

This deep sense of personal fragmentation is compounded by the all-pervasive sense of clutter that is a by-product of consumerism. Thoroughly indoctrinated by the messages of advertising, we seem destined to shop. And so we accumulate lots of stuff, not because we need it but because we are now so sure that it is necessary for our health, well-being, and happiness. Our lives become cluttered with bits and pieces that we hardly ever use. Clutter becomes a way of being, a state of mind. Sometimes, somewhere, someone stops and asks, "What is all this stuff for?" It doesn't all add up to significance or happiness.

It has now reached the point that the congestion of clutter has spawned a whole new industry specializing in simplifying the stuff of life. Mind over clutter. The clutter consultants have capitalized on a real desire to sweep out the inner clutter of life.

Desire for Wholeness, Holiness Today

In this cultural vacuum, the inner spiritual desire for wholeness reemerges with new energy and promise. As I see it, this desire for wholeness is our contemporary version of the search for holiness.

I am not suggesting that the shattered lives of refugees are to be easily compared to the cluttered lives of middle-class suburbia. However, I am suggesting that, from various perspectives, the desire for wholeness emerges as an important spiritual dynamic in this time and place.

This desire for wholeness permeates much of what is called the postmodern culture. This is a culture shaped by the suspicion of all forms of absolutism, by a rejection of "universal" worldviews, by a rebellion against imperialism in all its shapes and sizes. Although some forms of postmodernism can sometimes seem trite, there are other forms that resemble ancient prophetic critique: critique of idolatry, critique of the worship of political systems we have constructed, critique of the worship of the economics of silver and gold, and critique of the worship of imperialism in all its forms.

In his film *The Decline of the American Empire*, Quebec director Denys Arcand suggests the way of the Spirit in a place such as this. "We have no vision, no models or metaphors to live by. Only the saints and mystics live well at a time such as this."

To Concentrate a Life and Make It Whole

The shattering of various systems of meaning has left a vacuum that has created the space for a new desire for spirituality. The questions are: What form of spirituality? What form of holiness is appropriate for this moment? What can make our lives whole, can save us from the empire of the self?

This search for such a spirituality will have to begin with more modesty, more humility, with the willingness to accept the limitations of what is possible at an in-between time such as this. And to find this worthy and significant.

My reflections thus far suggest that we must listen for the calls that summon us out of our self-centeredness:

- The cry of a child.
- The call of the stranger and the newcomer focuses our lives.
- The call to do good work.
- The craft or art or sport that can discipline a life and shape it according to its material.

A spirituality that saves us from imperial religion will have to involve a spirituality of limits, of modesty and humility. This will not be easy, for it goes against some of our dearest dreams: the hope of becoming better, the hope of more, the hope of changing the world, the big hopes for the transformation of the church.

To become centered and focused is also to choose limitations, joyfully, willingly. It is the choice to locate your life. Not just for a moment but forever, it seems. Your life can no longer float around the universe, jet around the globe in the name of justice and peace or "the environment." It is easy to walk away from justice as a cause but much harder to walk away from the person who has knocked at the door.

Yet, is such a countercultural spirituality desirable? Is it possible? The sociologist Robert Bellah suggests that alternatives to the dominant culture must combine what is best in the culture with an alternative view.

One of the most persuasive articulations of a cultural alternative to fragmentation and clutter has been provided by the writer, thinker, and Appalachian farmer Wendell Berry. He is, according to the *New York Times*, "arguably the most prophetic voice in America today."

Berry was well on his way to a faster, better academic career as a writer. He traveled far and wide and often. Then he made the crucial decision to locate his life, his family, and his work in the small county of Port Royal in Kentucky. It is there that he has spent most of the last fifty years of his life, faithful to the land and the people of that small community. And in the process he has written almost forty books of essays, stories, and poetry.

It is there that he learned what it meant to be at peace and in place. It is there that he wrote his stinging critique of the expansionary views of empire. And he did so by drawing on some of the deep alternative roots in America—the words of the founding fathers of the republic, the words of Thoreau and others.

It was from this place that he criticized big government, which ran roughshod over the small farming communities in the name of progress. It was from that place that he criticized BIG ideas of economy and the environment that destroyed local land and local communities. In fact, he came to think of any big idea as a bad idea—because big ideas were lacking in affection for the local and real realities. He eschewed technology with its promise of a faster and faster life that left clutter and waste in its wake.

In the process he became the prophet of the local, a voice that anyone who thinks globally must come to grips with. Wendell Berry contended that if we do not know how to think locally, we will not know how to think globally.

There are indeed limits to Wendell Berry's view of the world. For example, the world that he writes from and about is strangely homogeneous. Although he writes about the value of welcoming the stranger, the strangers in all his writings look very much the same.

However, he has articulated a spirituality of limits that is compelling and persuasive. I have taught a course on Berry several times, and it is clear that his writings strike a deep chord with the students, most of whom have never lived in a rural setting, most of whom will never work on a farm. They find he speaks to the need and desire to be committed to a local reality, to a particular project. He speaks about virtues such as loyalty and affection, humility and fidelity and patience. These are traditional virtues, the virtues that make living and marriage and dying possible, and my students find them strangely refreshing and challenging.

What he has articulated is a spirituality of knowing our place in the world, in creation. It is a spirituality of being in place, of knowing one's particular contribution, of seeing oneself as part of something greater, as a participant rather than as a master and captain of the universe. He situates his life within a larger vision of faith and hope, but it only makes sense for Wendell Berry to the extent that it is concrete. The sense of choosing one's limits joyfully is also part of choosing the limits of love, of death.

This is not someone who is out to change the whole world. It is someone who remains faithful to a particular place and a people. It is a slow way. And it does make a difference.

There is one poem of Wendell Berry's that I think articulates both the postmodern experience of distraction and fragmentation and the corresponding search for wholeness. This search for wholeness is the search for holiness in our times. He called it the call to concentrate one's life. It is one of his Sabbath poems, written during the regular walks in the woods he takes every Sunday.

> *I walk on*
> *distracted by a letter accusing me*
> *of distraction, which distracts me*
> *only from the hundred things*
> *that would otherwise distract me*
> *from this whiteness, lightness,*
> *sweetness in the air. The mind*
> *is broken by the thousand*

calling voices it is always too late
to answer, and that is why it yearns
for some hard task, lifelong, longer
than life, to concentrate it
and make it whole.

—Wendell Berry, A *Timbered Choir*

Yet, one has only to read more of Wendell Berry to understand that he is not writing about a vague task, one that drifts off into abstraction and does not provide for the "concentration" of life. Essentially, what Berry is looking for is a way to "consecrate" his life, to commit and dedicate his life to that which is real, located, and concrete.

So Christians today have an opportunity to speak about meaning that is not identified with a particular political structure, but it must be meaningful in a way that is not abstract and vague.

A crucial bridge to this meaning is what the philosopher Albert Borgmann calls "focal practices," practices that bring one's life into focus, even when larger meanings still elude us. For example, the discipline of learning how to play a musical instrument brings an attunement of the self to the larger melodies; the regular practice of eating together can gather a family and community together even when the larger purpose of public gathering has become tenuous. The practice of the common meal draws the participants into a sense of community and sharpens the focus and purpose of those gathered.

I believe You
have given me
A word to speak
with my life.
This whole word
Concentrates my life
Gathers it up
and gives me over.
A burden no one
else can bear
A blessing no one
else can bestow.
O light burden
O heavy blessing
You are annunciations
Summons.
You call in me
and I call in You.
I call to You
I call with You.

Chapter 4

THE GOD OF SMALL NEIGHBORHOODS

Not in My Backyard

Behind one of the Romero Houses on Wanda Road is an old two-story garage, which may have had pretentions of coach-house grandeur at some earlier point in its history. It would probably be true to say that we bought this particular house because of the garage. The two large doors on the ground level were warped beyond the point of closing firmly, the shingles waved in the slightest wind, and wires hung helplessly from the mildewed walls. But it had space, generous and ample space.

We had developed a modest plan to renovate the dilapidated structure so that we could store donated food and clothes there and make space for a workshop where old furniture could be repaired. In bolder moments, we even envisioned that the top floor could become a place for arts and crafts with a corner for a sewing machine and weaving loom.

It was a modest dream, one that did not seem out of the realm of possibility. Slowly, over a period of three years, we raised money from various groups and individuals for this project. Finally, we were in a position to draw up some plans with an architect who was willing to help us for a fraction of his normal fee. He held a series of meetings at Romero House so the refugees could provide some input. Someone reminded him that the workshop should be separated from the rest of the building so the children wouldn't be tempted to play with the equipment. Another suggested that a second sewing machine would be more helpful than a loom. Those were exciting hours as we gathered around the long table on the porch, poring over the architect's designs. We were building something beautiful together.

All that remained, or so we thought, was to go through the committee of adjustment at city hall for all the necessary building permits. We did not foresee any difficulty because we had a letter from our next-door neighbor saying that the building had been used for storage and as a workshop over fifty years ago. Patrick was one of those rare persons who had lived on the same city block all his life. The letter meant that the garage renovations would not be hampered by the more recent city bylaws that had been designed to prevent the conversion of coach houses into rental units.

Pat and his wife, Mary, lived in full view of our large garage, which sat as a two-story wall along much of their backyard. They thought the plans for its renovation were sensible, long overdue. "It's going to collapse some day," Pat told me as he was watering the old grapevine that hung on a trellis near the garage. "If something isn't done, it's just going to fall down."

Georgia from across the street also liked the plan to renovate the garage. She had started working on crafts during the nights when she couldn't sleep for worrying about Peter, her disabled son. "I could teach the refugees some of the things I have learned once the craft area is set up," she said.

In retrospect, I think these were the only three neighbors we really knew during our first years on Wanda Road. We were simply too preoccupied with learning how to become good neighbors with the residents within our houses to pay too much attention to the neighbors outside. They were simply a backdrop to the life inside the houses. The street was just something we passed through on our way home.

There was only one neighbor I had not even seen—the man who lived two houses down from us. I had never noticed him, and I did not know his name.

All of the neighbors within two hundred feet of the garage received notice of the date the renovation project was to be presented to the committee of adjustment in early September 1995. None of the neighbors we knew were planning on going to the hearing because they thought the garage was a good idea and they assumed that everyone else thought it was a good idea. Little did we know that the neighbor without a name was preparing to do battle. He contacted all of his Eastern European friends from the street behind us and began to whip up a storm of protest.

The evening of the hearing at city hall, the chairman of our board presented the proposed changes to the garage. Earlier that afternoon he had sensed that there would be trouble when he had been accosted by the unknown neighbor.

"You people over there are just ripping the country off."

"We don't get any money out of this, you know. We're all volunteers."

"Like hell you are."

Lorne tried to contact the neighbors we knew to see if they could go to city hall to support us, but it was too late. They were either out of town or committed elsewhere. Only Pat Collins came.

The hearing began, and Lorne summoned up all the skills he had honed during his years as a high school principal. He launched into his presentation of the garage project, treading adroitly through the minefield of potential objections.

Then the unknown neighbor and twenty of his allies began to present their objections: the building would be raised twenty feet and it would make it easy for the peeping toms who were "over there"; there were wifebeaters at that house; there were wild parties going on at that house with lots of drinking; it would bring criminal elements into the neighborhood; there were too many children over there, people breeding like rabbits. Not in my backyard.

Pat fought back saying that this was not the case, that the garage wasn't to be raised; that the parties were quieter than most on the street; that there were good people in the house and that he should know because he lived next door.

It was too late. The committee sensed that much of the neighborhood was against the project and ruled against the renovations on a technicality.

The garage seemed to deteriorate slowly that fall. We could have appealed the ruling of the committee but we sensed that the unknown neighbors would make life even more difficult for the refugees. The money we had raised for the project was returned to those who had given it specifically for the renovation of the garage.

I was discouraged by the turn of events on Wanda Road just as I was disheartened by the mean spirit that was prowling around the political landscape. As I walked along the streets near our house that autumn, I noticed a lot of people who seemed to be Eastern European. I would look at the man raking his leaves, at the woman sitting on the porch, at the two men on the sidewalk talking in

Eastern European accents. And I wondered: *Was it you? Were you the one? Were you at the meeting?*

The questions built upon one another until I had constructed a wall between me and the unknown people on the block and in the streets around it. However, there was a crack in this wall, an insight just small enough for my soul to slip through. I realized that I was becoming like those I was fighting against. I had stopped thinking of these people as neighbors. I had become racist, indulging in a dangerous caricature of Eastern Europeans. I had begun to think of them as my enemies, and I had constructed a border within myself to keep them out.

I prayed: *Don't let me give up on us. May we meet again at the border.*

A few weeks before Christmas I received a phone call from some new neighbors on the corner, Mary and Keith Leckie who were both involved in film production. They felt their children received so much at Christmas and that it was important for them to learn about giving. Could their family bring presents for all the people in the Romero House on Wanda Road?

I went over to their house to discuss this thoughtful inquiry. As the Leckie kids roared in and out of the living room, Mary wondered whether they could know a little about each person in the house. What were their ages, their gender, their sizes, their interests? "You know we really are fortunate to have the refugees on our street," she said.

The words did not come easily. "It means a lot to hear you say that, Mary . . . especially after what happened to the garage."

"To the garage?"

I went back over what had happened earlier in the fall. Keith *was outraged and said, "That's terrible. You should have told us. We didn't know."*

"Perhaps that's what I've learned," I replied. "We have been so preoccupied with trying to live as good neighbors with the refugees that we haven't taken the people on the street seriously. They don't know us, and we don't know them. We see each other but we don't see each other."

"Well, you can't do everything," said Mary in her producer's voice. "Let's try and do something for Christmas."

And they did. The day before Christmas Mary and her kids arrived with boxes of presents and special food for each family. One of the little Sri Lankan girls clasped her hands in delight and said, "We have such wonderful neighbors here."

A Long and Daily Way of Life

This act of kindness strengthened our resolve to stay. Later that spring, Georgia held a barbecue for people on the street. The residents of Romero House were also invited, and it was the first time that many of us on the street learned each other's names. One woman, the wife of someone in the gang of twenty, went home to her husband and said, "There are some really nice people over in that house."

The acts of kindness seemed to gather unto each other like a snowball rolling down a hill. One of the young Latin American women at our house offered to help clean up the garden of an elderly couple on the street. When the couple brought out the money to pay her, she refused, saying that, in her culture, it was an honor to help the elderly. One of the African men, a very bored engineer who had never seen snow in his life before, began to shovel the sidewalk of the entire street. One of the neighbors offered to help get some of the new refugee kids registered at the school her children attended. Three of the houses on the street went together to purchase a snow blower that was then stored in the now infamous Romero House garage.

After we had lived about ten years on the street, a wonderful Portuguese couple from the Azores suggested that we have a street festival as a way of building a positive sense of neighborhood. They had memories of the time when the street had organized against the garage, and they wanted to ensure that nothing like that happened again.

I had a pretty simple picture of what a street party might look like—a few barbecues pulled out on the sidewalk and perhaps some music. However, Tony Rebelo was a true artist and an inventive builder to boot. He obtained all the decorations from a Portuguese festival in the city and built several archways over the street with lights and balloons so that the whole street seemed to resemble a small urban cathedral on that day. He built a stage for a talent show, invited the refugees to perform some of their own music, and organized a large potluck supper. Later that night the whole street rocked as we danced away our fears. It was splendid and became the first of an annual event on the street that now attracts several hundred people. Many of the former Romero House residents return at that time to connect with the wonderful neighbors they had met on that street. The Wanda Road Street Party has been the subject of several documentaries and feature articles that have described this as a neighborly model for welcoming the newcomers.

Over the next few years there were probably a thousand acts of kindness such as this, simple but real. I do not know exactly when, and I am not completely sure why, but at some point we became neighbors on that little street and in the surrounding blocks.

There are many books on community development, and I have read some of them. However, I now know that it does not work the way it is usually described in the books. The literature on community development makes it appear as if it is possible to go into an area, identify an issue, and organize around it, and voilà, a neighborhood. According to the experts, this can be done in a year or two.

Wrong and wrong. Building a neighborhood takes a very long time. It takes at least twenty years and then some. It takes every day. Like a garden, a neighborhood must be tended regularly and by many people There are seeds to be sown, little plants to water. And yes, every day there are weeds to be pulled, small problems to be solved before they overwhelm what is good. It is a humble task, and it is never over. There are days when you think the slightest storm could blow all this loveliness away.

Through the street party and many other gatherings, the neighbors came to recognize the Romero residents and learned their names. As they conversed together, the neighbors began to realize the immense talent and gifts that the refugees had brought. The refugees were no longer treated as a "social problem" but as a neighborhood asset. The neighbors began to find the first jobs for the refugees, the crucial first step in gaining the "experience" that would launch them into long-term jobs. Some of the neighbors were able to offer some translation services for the newcomers. Other neighbors helped get the refugee kids enrolled in various sports activities. Most important, there were neighbors who invited the refugees for a meal. Such an invitation accomplished far more than any official settlement program could do. The refugees felt welcomed as human beings, recognized as persons, each with a name and a face. They felt they could live in this place, could make a home, and find peace. I always waited for them to come home from such meals, to hear about every detail and to delight in the transformation that such a simple invitation had made.

It Takes a Neighborhood to Welcome a Refugee

As we began to reflect on our experience, we realized that the neighborhood itself was becoming the most important resource in helping resettle people who had been so harshly uprooted. Without planning it, we had grown into a model of welcoming refugees that was quite different from the usual agency model in which refugees were served by social workers and counselors. We did not have employment counselors; we had good neighbors with connections. We did not have translators; we had good neighbors who spoke languages other than English. We did not have child-care workers; we had good neighbors with kids. We did not have settlement workers; we had good neighbors who liked to cook and who enjoyed having company.

All of this was possible because the refugees were living in an ordinary neighborhood in which they came face to face with people who called this place home. We realized that, in spite of the best of intentions, many social policies keep the newcomers from meeting ordinary citizens. Taxpayers pay money to the government that in turn pays social workers to help "them." In the process "the taxpayers" and "the clients" never meet each other, never see each other face to face. People such as refugees are placed in shelters that are usually removed from residential areas. The distance between "us" and "them," the ghettos of poverty and the gated communities, becomes a vast indifference and can become a dangerous divide in times of social stress. Refugees remain "issues" or "problems" rather than people with names and faces.

We were learning, to paraphrase the well-known African proverb, that "it takes a neighborhood to welcome a refugee." This became our new maxim at Romero House and we began to make the process of contributing to the building of a good neighborhood a priority. We realized that helping to create a healthy, safe, and functioning neighborhood was the best way to welcome refugees.

However, it was also becoming clear that the refugees themselves were an important factor in the building of a good neighborhood. As someone on the street put it, "Those refugees made us a neighborhood."

It Takes a Stranger to Summon a Neighborhood

When we first moved to the area, we did so because the housing was cheap and because there was a mosque nearby, a health clinic, and an employment center. It was, at that time, a "no-name neighborhood." It was a place where we thought we could disappear. On the streets where we lived, very few people knew each other's names.

However, the arrival of refugees into that small area in fact summoned people to respond to their obvious needs: they had no winter clothes; they had to be taken to the hospital; they looked so sad. The refugees summoned us all to goodness and decency. In responding to the refugees, the neighbors began to talk to each other and to get to know each other. The refugees focused the energies of the people on the streets around us. At first, of course, this was because the refugees seemed to present a threat that summoned people together, but later it was the great need of the refugees that encouraged people to gather in a concerted response.

In the process, everyone won. As the neighbors began to talk and gather together, they realized that there was, on our block, an old woman with an alcoholic son, neither of whom was eating properly. She was not able to get Meals on Wheels because of the technicality that her son was in the same house and presumably could cook for her. When the neighbors realized her desperate situation, they began to bring over meals on a regular rotating basis. Romero House prepared the Christmas meal for the mother and son for many years.

"It takes a neighborhood to welcome a refugee; it also takes a stranger to summon a neighborhood."

This is now our neighborhood. It is not a perfect place, but we have a great affection for it. Wendell Berry describes the gracious imperfection of such a place. "What I saw now was the community imperfect and irresolute but held together by the frayed and always fraying, incomplete and yet ever-holding bonds of the various sorts of affection. . . . It was a community always disappointed in itself, disappointing its members, always trying to contain its divisions and gentle its meanness, always failing and yet always preserving a sort of will toward goodwill."

Local Knowledge

Gradually, Romero House became part of a process that involved meetings and consultations in the little pie-slice-shaped area. It was a geographical orphan that had always been treated as a small attachment to some of the larger and more defined neighborhoods. People began to realize that the area needed a name in order to be recognized and to make a political difference. After about two years we named ourselves The West Bend.

Romero House was involved in this process in simple ways like delivering flyers. We had lots of feet on the ground! It was a great way for the newcomers to become involved in the political process. Many of the meetings took place at our center, and I started to attend the West Bend meetings regularly. The steering committee was an amazing group of people who paid attention to all the nitty-gritty aspects that are essential in a real neighborhood: natural plants along a railway track, cleanup days, the development of bike paths and stoplights where they matter. Eventually we began to flex our muscle and organized meetings around proposed developments in the area.

One of the developments, a thin thirty-three-story corner building aptly called "The Giraffe," posed a direct threat to the Romero Center and the residents who lived above the storefront. It was not so much the height that posed such a threat, although that was distressing enough, it was the proposed exit and entrance for the estimated three hundred vehicles that would be parked under that building. The cars were to exit in the morning right into the pedestrian traffic and the streetcar turn lanes of one of the busiest subway stations in the city. The cars were to enter the building in the evening through the laneway that was shared by Romero House and twenty-three small businesses.

The developer commissioned a traffic study that used some specialized technology to calculate the various flows of vehicles and pedestrians. The consultant's study concluded that there were no major traffic problems with the proposed plan. The city also had its traffic officer review this plan. He visited the laneway with his own equipment and concluded that the flow of traffic would be efficient and practical.

The consultants, the official, and the developer all went home at night. They would probably never visit the neighborhood again once the building was finished.

Meanwhile, those of us who used the laneway every day knew one crucial fact that they had dismissed: that the laneway narrowed to six feet at one point, barely enough room for one car. We had called this space "The Narrows," and it was an intense point of friction as vehicles tried to enter or exit at the same time. Delivery trucks parked in the Narrows brought all traffic to a standstill. The Narrows became treacherous in the winter as vehicles skidded into each other. We also knew that there were forty-eight vehicles parked along that laneway, and sixty vehicles that would be exiting just as three hundred cars would be entering the laneway at night. Those of us who lived and worked along the laneway could easily imagine the impending disaster. The consultants, officials, and developers could not envision the damages that their plan entailed. The difference was that we lived there and cared about the place. We didn't go home at night. We had what Wendell Berry has called "local knowledge."

We took photos of the Narrows, measured the laneway in different spots, counted the vehicles going in an out. We wrote briefs on the basis of our local knowledge. It was during this time that I pasted a new motto on my computer: "The Way of the Termite." I felt we were all chomping away on this problem in a daily sort of way and that eventually the whole Giraffe building would just topple over.

We all wanted more people in the area so the small businesses could make a go of it but not at the cost of the safety of our neighbors, not at the price of fracturing relationships on a daily basis. At one point, some of the people in the neighborhood began to call me "Our Lady of the Laneway" as I had become so ferociously protective of the small buildings and little enterprises that were being overlooked by "The Giraffe." To an outsider this was an ugly laneway, with a hodgepodge of rickety buildings, walls covered with graffiti, and more than its share of garbage. Nevertheless, this was our place, and we had an affection for it. The mural that our residents had painted on the wall of our building had never been tagged by the local graffiti artists. At the end of the block, an elderly Chinese woman had created a most beautiful garden on a postage-stamp-sized piece of land. Beside her building, Giorgis the cobbler sat outside and played chess with people who wandered by. I felt they had found the secret of life on that little corner. All of this hodgepodge of beauty would be wrecked by the honking of angry motorists as they confronted each other at the Narrows.

The consultants and developers would leave as soon as the quick profit had been made. They would never have to live with the consequences of their plans, their studies, and models. It is the damage caused when you make decisions beyond the reach of your affection and loyalty. As Wendell Berry has written, although in the context of a local rural community, if you do not have an affection for a place you will not know how to think rightly about it.

We made our own assessment of the damage and we fought the Giraffe plan at city council and then, when the developer appealed this decision, we won again. It was the only time in years that a neighborhood had won against a developer in this large metropolitan area.

The struggle against Giraffe was not a Romero House struggle. It was a concern of a whole neighborhood, with many and various aspects to it, and we were part of it. After twenty years, we had become part of a neighborhood.

The Local and the Global

We had not become friends but we were no longer strangers and enemies. We had become neighbors. As I reflect on what has happened in this little neighborhood, it seems to me that it has significance for the post-9/11 world that we all live in. Becoming neighbors is a local project that has wider implications.

In political and social thought the world is often divided into those who are our friends and those who are strangers, between the world of the personal and the world of the political. We had learned that between familiarity and indifference there is still the possibility of neighborliness. This possibility has now emerged as newly significant in the world of political theory. This has been explored recently in an important collection of essays by Slavoj Zizek, Eric L. Santner, and Kenneth Reinhard, *The Neighbor: Three Inquiries in Political Theology.* "One problem with this account of the political, where we divide the world into friends we identify with and enemies we define ourselves against, is that it is fragile, liable to break down or even to invert and oscillate in the face of complex situations. . . . America today is desperately unsure about both its enemies and its friends, and hence deeply uncertain about itself."

On the morning of 9/11, we had just finished our morning team meeting at Romero House when a friend called to say we should turn on the TV. As the tape of the falling towers was played and replayed, various members of the team phoned those who were closest to them. I called friends of friends in New York City to see if there was news. The residents of Romero House, refugees from violent and war-torn situations, came into the common room and sat mutely watching the TV. I recall a young man from Algeria sitting silently on the couch, hands clasped tightly. He looked up at me, worry written all over his face: "What will happen to us now?" It was a question on everyone's mind: they knew there are recriminations for this kind of crime. And I thought to myself: "Everything will change." Empires under attack are dangerously violent. Any refugee will tell you this.

In the fall of 2001, one of the families in one of our houses was a Muslim family from Zanzibar. They had been forced to flee when the predominantly Christian government forces of Tanzania had refused to accept the results of the elections in Zanzibar. They had found a measure of peace at Romero House, and we came to respect Sauda, Jamal, and their three children. The oldest girl was a regal princess, the older boy was a budding genius with a geeky look, and the youngest son was just a happy kid. Behind the particular house that they were living in was a little park. Every day Jamal would take the two youngest kids there to play while the mother was attending English classes. They began to talk with some of the other young parents who came to the park. Jamal became friends with Matthew Stern and his wife, Caroline Newton, and their son, Noah. Matthew's mother had been a Jewish child in France who was hidden by a Catholic family during the time of the Nazi occupation. She was taken in on condition that she would not be raised as a Jew. Matthew wasn't really religious, but he identified himself as a Jew. When he learned of Jamal's computer engineering skills, he was able to get him a job at his company. Matthew went to Jamal and Sauda's refugee hearing and was profoundly moved when he learned what his neighbor had suffered in Zanzibar: imprisonment and torture that now made it impossible for him to play soccer.

On the morning of 9/11 Jamal felt stricken. He was ashamed, angry at what these so-called Muslims had done. He somehow felt responsible, and he didn't know why. He didn't know what to do that day. The interns heard him pacing back and forth in his room. Finally, around suppertime he went with Sauda and the children and knocked on the Sterns' door. When Matthew opened, Jamal looked down and said "I just wanted to say we are so sorry and I didn't know who to say this to." Matthew and his wife were just sitting down to begin supper. They invited Jamal and Sauda and the kids to join them at the table. So they all ate together, silently, sadly, but together.

I recall this story because it is a testimony to the possibility of peace among peoples. It also illustrates the near impossibility of such peace in a time when the violent actions and reactions of empire have been unleashed and laid bare for all to see.

Our faith has been profoundly intertwined with the realities of empire. By the time of Jesus, the image of the emperor was omnipresent—on every coin, in every building, in every decree. It was an empire that thrived on the spoils of war, that grew by dividing others into allies and enemies. What Jesus preached and how he lived and died struck at the foundations of empire. He bore witness to another way of being; he preached about the possibility of the reign of God rather than the rule of empire. In the time of Paul, the empire was still at the peak of its powers, and Paul urged the persecuted Christians of Rome to think about their lives and their world in a new way.

By 410 A.D. Christianity was no longer the religion of a persecuted minority but had become the religion of empire. Then as now, Christians pondered the significance of the shock of imperial mortality. Augustine spent thirteen years thinking about the significance of the fall of Rome.

Other writers have noted that the shift from being an empire in a process of development to becoming an empire in decline coincides with a fading of the original vision of the republic. The empire becomes less defined by a vision that it is for than by what it is against.

An empire in decline has a great need for enemies as the social glue that holds a society together. Since the 1950s, America has become increasingly defined by its enemies, by what it is against rather than by what it is for. During the long time of the Cold War, communism was the great enemy. Gradually, being American meant being anticommunist more than being for democracy. When this enemy fell, a number of lesser enemies such as Noriega of Panama failed to provide the necessary social glue. With the event of 9/11 the new and great enemy of Osama bin Laden emerged. Terrorism has become the great enemy. We know who and what we are against, sort of. But do we know what we are for?

It is into this cauldron of violent ideologies that the teaching of Jesus comes as a shock. "Love your enemies." To preach this, with our lives, is to strike at the heart of the imperial culture that we live in.

There is another way. This is a message that we must speak, not only to criticize but because we care. The present

obsession with the terrorist enemies is not only destroying
many innocent people: it is impoverishing the country; it
is legitimizing and minimizing the violence that runs deep
throughout gender and racial conflicts.

It is also destroying us spiritually. It is a sad and simple
truth that we become like what we fight against. It is simply
true that if we look at an enemy long enough we begin to
replicate its patterns within ourselves.

When we spent decades fighting the materialism and lack
of freedom in communism, we became more materialistic
and less democratic. So too, in fighting terrorism we become
more accustomed to disregarding the innocent, in justifying
torture.

This dynamic, in which we become like what we fight
against, is also (let us confess) present in groups working for
justice and peace. In our struggles against racism there is a
good chance we will become racist. We may struggle against
patriarchy and become more dogmatic than the pope. If we
are simply against violence, we are likely to replicate patterns
of violence within our groups. What a difference to be not
only against violence but also for peace.

So Jesus commanded us then as now to love our enemies.
He understood that otherwise we will become like the enemies we struggle against. His great hope and great promise
was that we would become like what we love. That if we love
God we will become more like God. If we love Jesus we will
become more like him. That if we desire the reign of God we
will begin to change our relationships, not because we have
to but because we want to.

However, enemies are essential within the imperial con-sciousness that pervades our culture. In the world of politics, other groups are divided into allies and enemies, evil empires and good empires. Within the world of the personal, relation-ships are divided into friends and enemies.

These great divides afflict our political and personal rela-tionships. Is it really possible to hope for peace among the peoples, for love between enemies?

Beyond Friends and Enemies

It is worth recalling that Jesus spoke not only about en-emies and friends; he also had a great deal to say about what it meant to be neighbors. This strikes me as a crucial form of relationship that helps us move toward responding to the apparently impossible challenge to love our enemies.

In her influential studies on the life of neighborhoods, Jane Jacobs said that neighborhoods function when people are nei-ther too close nor too far, not overly involved in each other's lives but not indifferent to each other. It means looking out for each other, sharing a common space; it involves proximity. It involves face-to-face relationships that go beyond the faceless world of the political AND the intimate and private world of family and friends. To live in the same neighborhood is not just a happening; it is also a choice. Jane Jacobs is actually the urban correlative of Wendell Berry. She examines the life of neighborhoods from below rather than from the lofty perch of urban planners. She concludes that the size and shape of a street is crucial to creating the right space between people.

Let me return to the story of Matthew and Jamal. They shared a common space, a little park, by choice and not simply by accident. In that face-to-face relationship the categories of Jews and Muslims broke down just as the face-to-face relationships at Romero House had broken down the categories of Muslims and Christians.

Neighborliness created a space beyond enmity. Jamal and Matthew were not friends, but there was respect, care, interest, which is a very long way from seeing each other as threat and enemy.

We should at least think what it might mean to live in proximity, near to, nearby, those who are different and other and strange to ourselves. This may mean geographical proximity, but it may also involve other forms of nearness. The very practical question of mixed-income housing is a crucial element in developing face-to-face relationships with those who are different from us.

The little park is a small space. A little wading pool, a sandbox, and some swings and slides. It is maintained by the parents and people who use it on a daily basis. Every year there is a little festival to raise money for equipment.

I pass this little park every day on the way over to the storefront that is our office. This small space reminds me that our work for peace in this particular empire should not attempt to replicate the patterns of empire. We should at least question the large plans, the big strategies, the global visions, and the wide connections that may subtly replicate the patterns of empire.

Chapter 5

SYSTEMS WITHOUT A FACE; FILES WITHOUT A NAME

Indifference

So much depends on whether we see another person face to face. So much depends on whether we know the name of the other person. As we see each other and learn each other's names, there is the possibility of becoming neighbors. There is even the possibility of love and perhaps hatred. However, indifference is no longer possible. The greatest problem in the world today is not so much hatred of those who are different from us but the vast ocean of indifference between us.

Indifference is not so much a character flaw, although it may be that too. Within this culture, a culture organized and sustained by various bureaucracies, we participate in organized indifference. We are both the victims and perpetrators of this indifference. The systematic indifference of bureaucracies renders us all faceless and nameless. Nobodies.

It is probably true to say that if we were all good neighbors, there would be no need for welfare systems, immigration systems, health-care systems, educational systems. We could live in the shelter of each other if we were all good neighbors. The reach of mercy and the desire for justice could take place on a smaller and more local scale. However, others argue that there are not enough good neighbors to go around, not enough expertise, not enough resources, and this means that we must develop systems to ensure that the needs of the many are provided for. Although a face-to-face encounter enables us to respond to the summons of another person, it still leaves us unable to respond to the needs of the many. It would seem that the bigger the system, the better. Size is an unquestioned value.

The Paper Weight

This is how Efim Tsirulnikov lost his face and his name. This is how someone can be crucified with paper. Bear with this story. The crucifixion is slow but sure.

Efim had arrived in Canada, via Israel, after the Chernobyl disaster. He and his wife and son had been exposed to high levels of radiation when the cloud containing nuclear contaminants dropped over their town of Minsk in Bylorussia. Because Efim was Jewish, he and his family were able to flee to Israel but were unable to stay there because the heat exacerbated the burning of their skin that had been seared by radiation. The Canadian refugee system did not then and does not now have a category to accept refugees at risk because of environmental tragedies.

However, Efim did have a slight possibility of being accepted as an immigrant because of his great skill at renovating historic buildings. Everything depended on his getting a work permit and having a job offer. He had already received several job offers, as many contractors in the city were working on the refurbishing of historical buildings.

In January 1994, Efim applied for a work permit. The application form asked for a medical exam but did not mention a fee. Efim indicated that he had already done a medical on May 7, 1993.

In February, Efim received a response from the immigration office in Toronto saying that a work permit could not be issued until "you and your dependents in Canada have been medically examined." He sent a copy of his medical examination to the office with another application for a work permit.

On March 3, 1994, Efim received a reply from Toronto immigration saying that the permit could not be issued until he sent a fee of $200 by certified check (to cover the cost of work permits for him and his wife) and until the "results of the medical examination had been received by the immigration officer." The response indicated that there was no problem with the photographs or fingerprints.

Efim went immediately to the Toronto office and asked where the medicals should be sent. He was given an address in Ottawa and told that it would take two months to process the medicals and that he could apply again at that time. He sent the originals of the medicals to the Ottawa address.

In May 1994, Efim received a letter from the office for immigration medicals in Ottawa saying that the x-rays were missing. Efim immediately sent the x-rays to Ottawa. He also contacted his doctor to see if there was any problem, and the doctor said the x-rays were completely clear. Efim phoned the immigration call center in Toronto to try to find out if the medicals had been processed yet.

In early July 1994, Efim sent a new application form for a work permit to the Toronto immigration office. He included in his application a copy of the registered letter certificate indicating that the x-rays had been sent to Ottawa in May 1994 and a certified check for $100. He explained that this was for his work permit because his wife wanted to complete a course before she began to work.

By the end of July he received a memo from Vegreville, the small town on the prairies where there was a huge immigration office that processed a wide variety of applications. The number of immigrants and refugees actually living in Vegreville, a small ranching town, was probably negligible. The memo said that his application had been received and that he would hear in four weeks.

On August 12, 1994, Efim received all of his application package back from Vegreville–except for the certified check for $100.00. The memo said that he had not sent the correct amount of money. "The correct fee for your application is $125.00. You submitted $100.00. . . . An additional $25.00 is required." Apparently the fee structure had changed since Efim's original application that had been sent eight months earlier. Efim immediately sent a certified check for $25 to Vegreville–in addition to his entire application package.

On August 15 and 22, faxes were sent from Romero House to the client service unit at the office in Vegreville, urging some action on the request for a work permit. One of his employers was still holding a job open for him.

On August 23, a woman with a real voice called Romero House from Vegreville to say that, according to the computer, the work permit had been delayed because of an incomplete medical. A fax was sent to Vegreville indicating that the medicals of Efim and his family and the x-rays had already been sent to Ottawa and that proof of postage was included. The name of the examining doctor was included in this fax. The next day Efim had another fax sent to Vegreville stating that he had contacted his doctor regarding the medicals. She said that she had never received any notification from Ottawa indicating that there was a problem with the medicals.

On September 13, 1994, Efim received a memo from Vegreville indicating that the "application for employment authorization" had been received on August 29. Presumably this was the application sent with the check for $25. The memo indicated he would be receiving a response in four weeks.

Then, on October 20, 1994, Efim received a form memo from Vegreville indicating that the work permit could not be issued until "you have been fingerprinted" and "you and your dependents in Canada have been medically examined." A handwritten note on the form read: "Advised by medical assessment unit in Ottawa that your medical expired before you completed the requirements."

Over the next few days, Efim's wife phoned the immigration call center in Toronto to find out where to get forms for a new medical examination. Natalia was a bright and spirited person who was gradually recovering from the effects of the Chernobyl radiation. Her lovely blond hair had grown back, but it had lost its curl.

After several phone calls, the receptionist said the medical forms would be sent in the mail. They did not arrive. At that point, the couple sought the assistance of their Member of Parliament. Mr. Flis and his assistant said they would fax Vegreville immediately. Two months passed, and the medical forms had still not arrived.

On January 2, 1995, almost a year after his first application for a work permit, Efim called the immigration call center and asked that the medical forms be sent. The receptionist said that she would see that a request form was sent to obtain the medical form. On January 5, 1995, the request form arrived, and Efim filled it out *that same day. That same day, Romero House faxed the local Toronto office, which had moved, to ask a program specialist to ensure that the medical package was sent to Efim. Four days later Efim and Natalia went to the local immigration office to see if they could obtain the medical forms. The officer at the wicket did not want to give them the medical forms. The couple kept showing her the letter from Vegreville. The officer said the medical couldn't possibly be expired. Finally the couple got the forms and were fingerprinted, again. The officer said that they would have to wait at least two months for the medicals to be processed in Ottawa.*

The couple and their son had their medicals done again on January 18, paying $260. The medicals were sent by the doctor on January 25.

During this time the employer, David Walsh, who wanted to hire Efim sent faxes to the immigration offices in Toronto and Vegreville. He stressed that the job was still open and that it was becoming urgent. He also contacted two Members of Parliament about the situation. We also contacted the Member of Parliament for the Vegreville area to try to get something moving. She was astounded when she saw the chronology of Efim's attempt to get a work permit so he could be legally employed.

By this time David Walsh was steaming. On January 25, 1995, he got through to someone at the Toronto call center and emphasized that the work permit was a matter of urgency. The officer he talked to said her number was 6104. He was told that only Efim could make an appointment and that he should call himself and ask for worker 6104. Efim and Natalia called the immigration telecenter that day and asked for worker 6104. Efim was told that he could not ask for specific workers and that he had to take whoever answered the phone. *The person who answered the phone said Efim would have to wait another two months and would have to fill out another form and that there was no faster way.*

On February 22, Efim received a letter from Immigration Canada with a sealed envelope inside. The letter said that the sealed envelope must be given to his doctor. Efim then went to his doctor with the envelope. The letter inside was a simple request for a TB skin test. On February 27, the results of the TB skin tests indicated positive and this was sent to Ottawa. The doctor had no concerns and explained to Efim that everyone from the former Soviet Union tested positive because everyone there had been immunized against TB and thus had been exposed to the germ. "Everyone responsible for immigration medicals knows this," he said. The doctor also pointed out that Efim's chest x-rays on two occasions had been completely clear.

Efim received a letter from Vegreville, dated April 18, saying that his medical was incomplete. The letter also said: "Please note that you will also have to submit $125.00 cost recovery as the money orders you submitted in 1994 are nonrefundable as your application for an employment authorization was refused at that time."

On April 24, the doctor sent a note to the immigration medical assessment unit indicating that the results of the TB skin test had been sent by UPS courier to Ottawa on March 1. The doctor explained that all people from the former Soviet Union test positive for TB because of the state practice of inoculation.

The next day, Efim received another letter instructing him to take the sealed letter to his doctor. Inside was a directive for Efim to take a sputum smear for TB to be incubated for six to eight weeks and to repeat a chest x-ray before and after the sputum test. At this point Natalia lost it. She threw up her hands and began screaming, "By *the time we are allowed to work in this country we will be mentally retired!"*

Efim plodded on and went to have the sputum test that day, but the doctor told him that Efim should not have any more x-rays. People who had been exposed to high levels of radiation during the Chernobyl disaster, he said, were not to have more than one x-ray a year.

The work permit was so near and yet so far. Efim and his family were running out of time to apply for permanent residence on humanitarian grounds. In desperation I flew to Ottawa for a personal meeting with the parliamentary secretary for citizenship and immigration. I had sent her all the documentation relating to this Kafkaesque situation.

She told me that she had asked the departmental officials to explain why there had been such a delay in getting a work permit. "You know what they said? They said this man had shown no evidence of having made a serious effort to get a job."

No one ever apologized. The system remained infallible.

No one had to face the frantic couple who felt that their lives were being filed away forever. There was no one to blame and no one to ask for help. In the end the parliamentary secretary came through, and Efim received his work permit. I think this happened because I knew her name, and she knew mine. I had gone to see her face to face in one last desperate attempt to keep them from disappearing into a hole of oblivion.

"Mary," I had said to her. "We need this family here. It is not simply because he is a skilled worker. We also need them to remind us that nuclear disasters are real, that they have happened, and that real people suffer because of these accidents. We need them as witnesses."

Efim began to work and more or less got on with his life. He died this year, of cancer. I believe he saw God face to face. I believe that God called him by name.

I thought about all the officers at the wickets, the receptionists at the end of the phone line, the distant deciders in a small town on the prairie. What were they like? Did they go home at night to the kids? What were their names? Did they enjoy their work? Did they ever realize the devastation caused by their collective indifference?

These people were probably rather decent. If they had ever met Efim and Natalia, they would have been moved to compassion. They would have been horrified to see how they turned pink in the heat and how their son still had a bluish tinge to his face. I imagine they would have admired Efim's inventiveness and delighted in Natalia's wicked sense of humor.

I had a hunch that many of these people went to church in that little prairie town and that they were good parents.

Nevertheless, they had all participated in the wreckage. And they did not know it. And we did not know who they were.

Systematic Evil

We had come up against the reality of systematic evil, the kind of system that shuffles off mercy, muffles the cry for justice, and renders people invisible.

This type of evil is experienced not only by refugees. It is experienced often and by many who have to deal with various types of systems: an elderly couple trying to access medical care; a family trying to contact someone about their unemployment insurance; people led down garden paths; the homeowner who tries to speak to someone, anyone, at the bank who can renegotiate his mortgage.

Systems supposedly designed to do good develop routines of indifference, procedures for acceptable cruelty.

I have talked with many church people who have become companions to real people called refugees. They begin to see the immigration system (and other systems such as the welfare and health systems) through different eyes.

These systems seem designed to deface human beings, to separate us from each other and from ourselves. This is a social and religious shock for the Christian who now knows the refugee by name, who now sees the face as the landscape of one particular history. This person has been given a client ID number and has been filed away. From time to time pro forma letters arrive to signal that another hurdle has been passed and that the end, the place of safety, has been reached.

However, sometimes the letter says. "You have been determined not to be a Convention Refugee." And then, "You have fifteen days to present yourself at the Immigration Detention Center." Case closed. Another life is filed away.

The immigration officer who issued the form letter never has to see the hand that trembles after the envelope is opened. The church worker sees and is afraid.

Sometimes this fear galvanizes a whole church community into action. Then comes the long time of letters and visits to politicians. A sense of futility grips those of little faith.

This is the time of temptation. It is all too easy to begin to demonize "the system" or particular people who are supposedly in charge of the system. It is tempting to engage in the struggle of US against THEM and indeed such a struggle tends to attract people inclined to this contemporary form of Manichean dualism. WE are right and THEY are wrong. WE are on the side of the angels against the unjust and deceiving enemies.

The authentically Christian response, in the midst of this struggle, is to remain life-size. The church worker who now knows the real refugee, who is neither better nor worse than the conventional stereotype, must resist the temptation to demonize immigration officials and/or politicians. The Christian must preach (in action more than words) that the employees of the system are also human and must be summoned to life-size responsibility.

There is indeed something demonic in this situation, but it is not the officials in the system but rather the system itself. The reflections of the political thinker Hannah Arendt on bureaucratic systems are as relevant today as they were more than fifty years ago. In her efforts to understand the conditions that made the Holocaust possible, she described the ways in which ordinary people doing a good job could contribute to evil of great consequence—without ever knowing it or willing it—because the system acted as a buffer between their intentions and the consequences of their actions. Bureaucracies, in her analysis, are structured in such a way that it seems as if nobody is responsible for the terrible consequences of their cumulative action—not those on the top, who never see the people affected by their decisions; not those on the bottom, who see the people but experience themselves as helpless victims. Those on the top can argue that they never really killed anyone, while those on the bottom can say that they were only following the orders of someone else. The systems are organized so that everyone is somewhat implicated, but no one feels responsible.

Nevertheless, such systems wreak horrible havoc. When I visited Auschwitz for the first time earlier this year, I was overwhelmed by the scale of this concentration camp. No photograph can convey the sheer size and scale of this city of organized murder. It took thousands upon thousands of people to plan, organize, and execute the genocide of European Jewry. It was not hidden away in some field but covered a vast stretch of land in plain view.

Many saw and did not see. There were murderers among the Nazis to be sure, but they were able to accomplish their goals only because of the immense indifference of so many.

Arendt makes the important observation that in some medieval paintings the devil has a mask. He is the faceless one, the Nobody. In the various systems that hold the power of life and death over refugees, it often seems that NOBODY is responsible. Refugees who arrive in the West know what happens when NOBODY is responsible. NOBODY can kill you just as anybody or somebody can.

One of the challenges involved in working with refugees is to summon all concerned to face themselves. It is an act of ethical resistance to say systems have been created by human beings and therefore can be changed by human beings; systems must be changed so that human beings can face each other and face the consequences of their actions. For the church worker who knows a refugee as a person, this is not an abstract ethical statement about what ought to be done. It is the stubborn statement of someone who holds another by the hand and trembles.

Those of us who are more familiar with the structures of the Roman Catholic Church are often slightly confused by this bureaucratic form of sinfulness. We are used to the good old-fashioned form of hierarchical organization in which it is clear who is on top of the organization and who is responsible. The pope and the bishops have a face and a name, and, for better or worse, they bear responsibility. Somebody can be praised or blamed.

However, the reality is that most people in North America live and move within systems of indifference in which no one seems responsible. Hannah Arendt described it as an "onion structure" in which there are layers upon layers with nothing and no one in the center. This is profoundly disempowering for all those who are drawn into this vapid type of system.

So much depends on whether we can develop the social forms in which people can meet each other face to face. So much depends on whether we can face ourselves. So much depends on whether we can see the consequences of our own actions.

There may be those called to create alternative forms of human mercy and justice. There may be others who feel called to change these systems from within, and there may be others who work together to develop spaces within systems where face-to-face interaction is possible.

Chapter 6

THE IN-BETWEEN CHRIST

Living side by side with refugees gave me a new sense of the differences that defined us. However, it also shattered the layers of indifference that had encrusted our hearts. In some mysterious way, it was in living with people from different cultures and religions that I became more definite in my own faith, more definitely Christian.

Sir George and the Sheik

He seemed rather tall, even patrician, when he first arrived with his arms flung over the shoulders of his two friends. His sharp features were almost tragically set off by his half-shaved head and the shock of long black hair that covered what looked to be a good eye. A large black eye patch covered much of the other side of his face. "His name is George," said one of his friends.

"Sir George to you," he said as he tossed back his hair and winked with his good eye. "So what kind of service does this establishment have to offer?"

Sir George had obviously fallen on hard times. His two friends had found him in a coma in a rundown basement apartment and had called a shelter, whose representative then called us to see if we could take a dying man from Sri Lanka.

"Tell me more," I replied.

I learned that George had been a highly educated and successful naval engineer in Sri Lanka. He was not really involved in politics and was more interested in wine, women, and song. Eventually he married Marina and more or less settled down to a comfortable life in a large house with servants. They named their first daughter Maria Lourdes because they had visited Lourdes on their honeymoon to France.

His problems started with the stupid fact that as a teenager he had engaged in some rather foolish antics that resulted in his agreement to have someone tattoo a small tiger on the left cheek of his behind. His friends jokingly called him "Tiger." It was an innocent term of endearment but it soon became a dangerous designation in Sri Lanka when the Tamil Tigers (LTTE) began their struggle against the Sinhalese majority in Sri Lanka. All Tamils became suspect, not only those who were militant.

All it took was one night in a bar when a drunken friend yelled across to George, "Hey, Tiger!" Someone must have reported the incident because the police soon arrived and took George away for questioning. They discovered, in the course of stripping him, the tattoo of the Tiger. He was beaten severely. An iron bar was pushed through one of his eyes and into his head. Only a hefty bribe paid by his family secured his release. He knew it was simply a matter of time before he would be picked up again.

Fearful for his life, he found a job as an engineer on an ocean liner and traveled around the world until he reached Montreal. From there he took a train to claim refugee status in Toronto.

He was accepted quickly and found a job as a translator. About two months after taking this job he became increasingly dizzy; his speech was slurred, and he became confused in his work. When he collapsed in the midst of translating for a refugee lawyer, he was taken to the hospital where he was diagnosed as having a cancerous brain tumor. It was not clear whether there was any relationship between the tumor and the iron bar that had been driven through his eye into his head. The surgeons operated immediately, apparently without much success.

Because of hospital cutbacks, George was released soon after his operation and sent to a shelter for homeless men to recover. There he was surrounded by drug addicts and alcoholics. His belongings were locked up, and he was forced to walk the cold streets during the day. One night he was beaten by the man sleeping next to him. Desperate, he collected his papers and used what little money he had left to get a basement room in a boardinghouse. He had just enough strength to make one last phone call, giving his address. Alone, he lapsed into a coma until his friends arrived.

I knew we had a room in our house that had only recently become vacant. It was the room next to mine. I knew that accepting George would involve a lot of care, and I sensed that we could not do it unless everyone in the house agreed.

We called a meeting of all the residents in our house and invited a nurse from a local clinic. At that time the house was entirely Muslim with the exception of me. There were two Eritrean women, Samara and Zeinab, each a single mother with several children, and Mohammed, a captain in the Somali army who had recently arrived with his wife, Lul.

The nurse explained to all of us the implications of accepting

George—how he would slowly or quickly deteriorate, how he would soon be unable to move from his bed, how he would need help with all the basic things in life, like eating and going to the bathroom. I asked everyone to think about whether we could make such a commitment.

"I say yes," said Samara. "He has no family. He has no home. We each do some. In our country, sick person stay home. Hospital no home. We family now." Everyone else nodded and preparations began in earnest.

We set up a schedule so that each of the adults in the house would take a turn at cooking and cleaning for George once a week. We offered to find some money to reimburse them for the cost of the food, but they would have none of it. They insisted on sharing what little they had with someone who was dying. Some of our friends in the neighborhood helped with the bathing.

He needed all of this and more. Indeed, he insisted on more. The more physically helpless George became, the more demanding he became. Somehow the other women in the house seemed to understand. "Must talk strong because no strong now." They patiently prepared his meals and often sat to talk with him as he was eating. He was not grateful.

One day I overhead George shouting at Samara who had brought him supper, "Your English leaves a little to be desired, my dear. Is that Muslim food?" he asked as he poked around the plate. I was furious. I walked into his room and lambasted him: "This is not Sri Lanka, and these women are not your servants. Stop snapping your fingers, and start saying please and thank you. They know what it is to have servants of their own. There are no more servants here, just neighbors."

"He sick, Mary Jo. It's okay," said Samara.

"Yes, I'm sick, Mary Jo, and don't you forget it."

How could I? My part of this bargain-basement care was to help George during the night. He had a little bell by his bed, and he would ring two or three times a night when he had to go to the bathroom. He liked ringing bells, my bells.

At first it was not that difficult. I would walk beside him until he reached the bathroom. From there on he was assisted by the handrails we had installed by the toilet. Soon I had to hold him by the arm, and then I had to pull his arm over my shoulder and pull him along the hallway. He felt heavier and heavier.

Sometimes we would chat when he was finally back in his bed. His mind would wander.

"I'm a son of a bitch, you know."

"I know."

"Do you think I'll go to hell?"

"Probably not. You'd expect more service than they usually offer there."

"I have a bottle of holy water from Lourdes in my suitcase. Could you sprinkle some on me? It can't do any harm. I'd love to see my daughters before I die. By the way Jo, you've got a great future as a night nurse."

Finally one night I couldn't lift George out of bed any more. A tear formed in the corner of his good eye. "I'm wet." That's all he could say as he lay there quietly.

I could hear the sound of Mohammed upstairs on the third floor, chanting his prayers. I had been a little nervous when he first arrived not because he was a Muslim but because he was a sheik and had been a captain in the Somali army. I didn't know what that meant, but I did know that two or three times a night he would rise to pray because, as he said in good English, "When all the world is silent, that is when Allah hears our prayers more easily." It made me feel like a bit of a spiritual slouch.

I was aware that night that how I dressed and acted was mostly "haram" or unclean to Sheik Mohammed. He would not shake my hand when I reached out because it was "haram" to touch a woman's hand. I did not cover my head and arms. Haram. And that night when George wet his bed I was dressed only in my pajamas.

Nonetheless, I decided to go upstairs to knock at Mohammed's door. "Please help me. Help George, bathroom."

"Yes," he replied instantly. He came down in his sarong and together we hauled George to the bathroom. Every night thereafter, whenever George would ring his bell, Mohammed would come down to help us. He explained to me that it was more important to care for the sick and the dying than to worry about haram.

Then came the night when the bell did not ring. I woke up almost out of habit and went to get Mohammed. Neither he nor I could lift George, and we could not wake him. In the early hours of that morning we called the ambulance. As the paramedics brought him downstairs on a stretcher, everyone in the house, the women and all their children, Sheik Mohammed and Lul and I gathered by the door in our nightclothes. An immense sadness followed as our dear Sir George left the home he had called into being.

George lived only two weeks after that night. He was buried in a cemetery to the north of the city in a section reserved for indigents. All of George's neighbors from Romero House accompanied him

there. As we were driving home from the cemetery, Samara asked
me, "What means sunbeech?"

"Sunbeech?"

"Yes. He say all time I'm sunbeech."

I let the word roll over in my mind. "It means he was a good man
but he didn't know it."

The long nights with Sir George and Sheik Mohammed
and the days spent with Samara and Zeinib were some of
my most formative experiences as a Christian. In ways that I
can hardly articulate, even years later, it was with them that
I understood what it meant to be a follower of Christ. I had
learned the most important things about suffering and love
and service from my neighbors who were not Christian. These
strangers called me home.

A Summons to Faith

Many of my friends, aware of all the people from different
religions that I have lived with, have often asked me whether
it challenges my faith. My faith has been challenged, I reply,
but not because of the different religions at Romero House.
It has been challenged by the immensity of suffering, by the
great sense of powerlessness, and by the mute indifference
of the systems that we have to work within. However, I also
know that my faith has been strengthened by those whose
faith was different from mine.

Let me situate the reflections that follow. The religious be-
liefs of the residents of Romero House are many and various.
There are Hindus, Buddhists, Jews, Evangelical Christians,

Catholics, Alevis, Zoroastrians, Amaddhi Muslims, Sunnis, Shiites, Anglicans, Russian Orthodox, Jehovah's Witnesses, Seventh Day Adventists, Mennonites, and so on. Our policy at Romero House is never to engage in the process of trying to convert any of our residents. The simple reason for this policy is that so many of our residents have had to flee their countries because of religious persecution. We want to provide a space of safety in which the residents do not have to apologize for their religion or defend it. The residents are told about this policy as soon as they arrive, and it is made clear to all of our staff and interns. The residents are immensely relieved to hear about this policy, although a few of them still wonder if we are out to convert them.

We do explain to the residents that our work and service is inspired by our Christian commitment. Our interns come from many Christian denominations: United Methodist, Lutheran, Baptist, Mennonite, Anglican, Catholic, Evangelical, and Old Apostolic. There are also interns who are simply seeking to live a good and just life.

One would think that this is just an easy recipe for religious tolerance. One would think it would dilute various specific commitments in the general mix of things at Romero House. Everyone is asked to respect those who are different. This is true in obvious ways. We try to celebrate as many of the different religious feast days as possible. The Hindu Diwali, the Norooz celebration of the New Year, Eid, and Ramadan and, of course Christmas. On Christmas eve we have a Catholic liturgy, and, the next evening, we have an evening of peace to which all people regardless of their religious convictions are invited. It is a modest gathering of over two hundred people with many turkeys cooked in a variety of cultural ways.

As noted, it looks like an easy recipe for liberal tolerance. However, my experience is that living with such differences has, in fact, made me and many others more intensely committed and defined by our own traditions. It is as if living with the one who is different from us, who believes differently from us, has made us more ourselves.

On the simplest level, my neighbors have pointed out some of the distinctiveness of Christianity that I had not noticed before. Perhaps I had taken them for granted; perhaps they were too familiar. For example, Samara said to me that she was surprised that our neighbors had kept their severely disabled son, Peter, at home. She was astounded when we put in a ramp to make it easier for us to welcome refugees who were crippled or disabled. Through her ears, I heard that there are words of the gospel that have shaped us far more than we know—about the least of these, about the one who is lost, about who would be the greatest. It takes someone else to point out that the words that you have heard rattled off so often in church have actually become part of the being of a community and even the being of a church. Through the eyes of a stranger, I saw that my faith had grown in a culture of care and of mercy that is indeed astounding. It is indeed Good News.

There are also times when some of our residents, in explaining their own religious practices, have cast light on my own practices and let me see them anew. I am always moved during Ramadan by the powerful commitment of my Muslim neighbors. "The purpose of fasting," as Samara explained to me, "is to remember our hunger for God and to be mindful of those who are hungry." I began to rethink some of our Christian practices around fasting that we have so easily and quickly cast aside.

Some of my neighbors also explained the Muslim practice of doing something in secret, of doing a kind act in a way that no one will know you did it and no one will praise you for it. There is a similar tradition in Judaism and also in other religions. It made me aware in a fresh way that Jesus also tells us to pray in secret, to do good deeds in secret. This is an invitation to move beyond a contractual form of relating in which there is always some form of recompense whether monetary or simple forms of gratitude. The deepest and freest relationships are those in which we do something for nothing, for no reason: when we love God for nothing, when we care for another person for no reason.

The willingness of the Muslims to pray five times a day is also very impressive. No matter where they are they seek a way of reorienting their lives to God. There are other similarities that one discovers, like the story of the Prodigal Son. I recall a conversation with some Muslim parents who were concerned about their eldest son. When I told them the story of the prodigal son, as a way of encouraging them, they told me there was a similar story in their tradition and that it was important for the oldest son to know that he could always come home and that he would be welcome.

Yet, all of this seems simply like learning new information as you encounter a different culture, a different reality. It is interesting. It is valuable, and it broadens your horizons. It is the kind of information that can make you a more tolerant person.

The In-Between Christ

However, there is another level of transformation that can take place below and through this information. In my experience, Christ comes alive along the border between what is known and unknown, the familiar and the strange, the same and the different.

The border is the in-between space where Christ summons us today. This is where Christ breaks through our predictable pictures of God, our near-perfect theological notions, and our comfortable spiritualities. To discover this living Christ we must let go of the familiar Christ, and we must also let go of our idea that those who are strangers are so different from us that we have no concern for them. We must let go of the belief that our task is to take the Christ in our church and in our culture to those who are different. And we must go beyond the belief that Christ is already somehow implicitly in other cultures and faiths. This is the challenge that underlies most discussions of mission work today.

This challenge is similar to that faced by those who work with "the poor." Is Christ someone that I bring to the service of those who are poor, or does Christ exist in the poor and my task is to discover him and serve him in the poor?

In other words, is Christ on one side of the border or the other? Is Christ in us or implicitly in them? As we pose the question in this way, Christ seems like a frozen image that is in one place or another, here or there, in one culture or another, in one person or another. Christ seems like an icon that we bring to show another culture or like an icon hidden behind the face of someone who is different, a different culture, a different religion. Is Christ IN us or IN the poor? And what spiritual contortions we go through when we try to SEE Christ in the poor! It is sometimes very difficult to see Christ in the poor if the person has been defaced by poverty and injustice. Poor people are not always pretty.

My sense is that Christ is neither IN us nor IN them. Christ is alive along the border between us and them. The border between us and them, here and there, is where the Holy Spirit moves like breath, like breathing. The border is where the Spirit of Christ is activated, where the Spirit lives now, not only in the past or some distant future. The Spirit of Christ is born between us as we live together, suffer together, and rejoice together. Christ comes alive when another summons us to become who we really are. We become ourselves for the other.

My Muslim neighbors do not want me to become a Muslim. They want me to become a good Christian; they need me to become a good and responsible person. They trust those who believe; they trust those who trust in faith, who believe and hope. They trust those who will do something for nothing. And I trust a devout Muslim far more than a tolerant liberal.

Christ is born in the in-between; in the in-between of every relationship. As he said, "Where two or three are gathered."

He is present then as the energy that is activated through relationship, in the in-between spaces of life. Christ lives along the border that we cross and recross everyday as compassion and need meet and summon each other to justice and peace.

It is interesting to note that Jesus of Nazareth was summoned to a full awareness of his mission by a stranger, by the Canaanite woman (Mt. 15:21–28). The story of her great love for her daughter and her great faith is a turning point in the Gospel of Matthew because this foreigner, this woman, summons Jesus to a fuller understanding of his mission, that he has been sent not only for his own people but also for the strangers and foreigners.

A story: one of our interns, Jacob, was not given to wild religious sentiment. He was a careful, caring Mennonite, steady and humble in his faith. One day a young Iranian man arrived at our house. He was young, and he was gay and had barely escaped with his life from that country. He had been a Muslim, but his faith had been shaken by the mullahs who had preached such hatred against those who were gay.

He and Jacob began to talk in the evenings. One night Jacob noticed that Tariq was in great pain, and Jacob asked him what had happened. The young Iranian man took off his shirt and turned around so Jacob could see his back. It was covered with huge welts, whip marks, and open sores. "They beat me," said Tariq.

It was a moment of revelation for Jacob, not only about Tariq but also about Christ, who was suffering today. Christ was alive in that moment of revelation between Jacob and Tariq. Christ lived as compassion met suffering.

A Postmodern Spirituality

In the long history of Christian spirituality, the wise ones have taught us several ways to find the living God. There are spiritualities that emphasize discovering Christ within. Thomas Merton was the great contemporary guide along the path of discovering the true self. Others would call this the path to authenticity. There are certain conditions for this type of spirituality: deep silence, a withdrawal from busyness and clutter, the disciplines of a centered life.

Other types of spirituality emphasize discovering Christ in the world about us. Ignatius's desire to find God in all things has found many and various expressions in spirituality. This path presumes an involvement and engagement with the world and a method for discerning the presence or absence of God.

The kind of spirituality I have been attempting to describe is the discovery of Christ as our spirits are awakened by something or someone entirely other than ourselves. One could call this a postmodern spirituality.

Boundaries and Borders

At the heart of this spirituality is the issue of borders and boundaries, a personal and a political issue. There are those who uphold boundaries as a way of asserting or maintaining the identity of a group, race, religion, or nation. This use of boundaries or borders can become a way for a group to exclude others who are not like them. It is because of this that others reject all types of boundaries and borders because of their exclusionary use.

However, as some feminist thinkers have reminded us, some type of personal boundary is essential to personal identity if one is not to become overwhelmed by the identities of others. As other postcolonial thinkers have argued, some form of national or group boundary is necessary, or smaller political and social groupings will become overwhelmed by the realities of empire and globalization.

Everything depends on whether the border is defined by what a group is for or by what and whom it is against. Is the boundary drawn because of shared commitments or because of a common desire to exclude? Identity must involve some type of boundary between the self and the world, between one group and another. However, the boundary becomes destructive and dehumanizing if it is based primarily on the desire to exclude. Refugees know the difference between boundaries that include and those that exclude. We need to learn how to live along borders, how to think along borders.

Where Deep Joy Meets the Deep Suffering of the World

The spirituality that is summoned as the self meets the other has been finely described by the great Protestant writer Frederick Buechner in his oft-repeated statement: "The Place where God calls you is the place where your deep joy meets the deep suffering of the world."

Buechner is not only naming the dynamic that happens when something deep within connects with something deep without; he is also naming the sign of the authenticity of that connection, which is joy. To discern the presence of Christ we need to look for that mysterious gospel sign of joy in the midst of suffering.

There is a marvelous image of this sign in the little village of Xavier in the Basque area of Spain. This is the place where Francis Xavier was born and where he grew up. In the small chapel of the castle he called home, there is a large crucifix called "The Smiling Christ." No one knows who sculpted this crucifix, but it is thought that this crucifix took shape during one of the darkest periods in the history of Europe, the time of the Black Death and the calamitous corruption of the church in the fourteenth century. This was a time of great suffering and spiritual confusion. This context is evident on the side walls of the chapel: they are filled with skeletons doing the Dance of Death. And yet. And yet. Christ is smiling in the midst of his own suffering and the suffering of the dark age of Europe. When we can smile like that, we know we are where we are meant to be.

Many of our contemporary spiritualities seem to emphasize either joy or suffering. On the one hand, there are books that seem to suggest that we can live on an island of joy in the midst of a sea of suffering: turn off the news, start a garden, create a quiet spot, listen to calming music. On the other hand, there is more than enough information about the vast sea of suffering in the world. Spiritualities that respond to this reality are usually critical of social realities and articulate a vision of solidarity and hope. Nevertheless, many of those who work to alleviate some of the unnecessary suffering in the world are eventually swamped by the waves of cruelty and injustice.

The secular strategy for coping with this problem is to establish a "distance" or a boundary between oneself and the suffering of the world. On one side of the boundary is the suffering person, and on the other side is the caregiver. The person on one side becomes a client, and the person on the other side is a professional.

There is some wisdom in establishing this kind of relationship if it is the only way to keep the suffering of another from swamping oneself. However, there is a heavy price to be paid in such a strategy for dealing with suffering. The client is reduced to his or her particular problem, and the professional never gets to meet the multifaceted reality of the person they are trying to help. The caregiver, the advocate, the social worker never actually meets the complex reality of the person, who may have a wacky sense of humor, who loves his kids, who has secret dreams of going ice fishing in the winter, who is immensely resilient, who knows where to get wine cheap. In short, they miss the possibility that the client can be a source of joy and happiness and hope.

One wonders how much professional care is a sad substitute for the recognition by a neighbor, the help of a friend.

So many of our systems of "helping" in fact serve to distance people from one another, to prevent us from seeing the face and hearing the voice of the other person. We classify others as "issues" or "problems" or "cases" and so deface them in the process. Even with the best of intentions.

Yet, to really face another person who is in great suffering is to live with great risk. The suffering can be overwhelming and can lead to feelings of great powerlessness. It can touch off things within us, the places where we have been whipped and beaten.

It is easy to keep busy, to deny, to escape.

It seems like a risky way to live, and it is—unless, unless—we remember that there is a third person in the equation. It is not only me and the refugee; it is not only me and the child; it is not simply me the caregiver and the client. The poet T. S. Eliot described this mysterious presence:

> *Who is the third who walks always beside you?*
> *When I count, there are only you and I together*
> *But when I look ahead up the white road*
> *There is always another one walking beside you*
> *Gliding wrapt in a brown mantle, hooded*
> *I do not know whether a man or a woman*
> *—But who is this on the other side of you?*
>   —T. S. Eliot, *The Waste Land*

There is the Spirit in-between us, walking along the border. There is the Christ who lives between us and sustains us both. I think the most important thing we can do at the beginning and the ending of the day is to place all those whom we will meet that day and ourselves into the hands of Christ, who holds us and sustains us both. And at the end of the day turn over all the cares, works, and sufferings of the day into the hands of Christ. Then go to sleep in peace.

So much depends on whether we can learn to live along the borders, in the in-between spaces of life. At times it is an exciting place to be, a creative and sometimes dangerous place to be. However, more often than not it is a place to wait, a place to contemplate.

Being Still at the Border

The two women pause and gather their lives up in this single moment. They do not look at each other. They close their eyes and look within, behind and ahead. They stand still, between all that has been and all that shall be. This is the rarest of moments in the rush that picks a life up and pushes it forward.

It is the time of ingathering—all those loose ends, the dropped threads of their lives, the unraveling of relationships, the frayed edges of meaning. In the stillness the thin thread of life lengthens, slightly.

It is the time when the women, perhaps refugee women, have come to the edge of all that they have known, all that they have been. They gather up their lives, gather up who they have become, and prepare for the walk into the unknown. Will they find a place to land? Will they be given wings?

It is the time between countries, between lives, between people. The border of stillness.

Before this moment, there was the loud crying task of giving life, the buzz of bearing with, of bringing forth the little innocents. There were the songs for the small ones who slept, and there was the yelling and screaming, the warnings of danger just around the corner. Before this moment, there was the long sorrow that had to be kept quiet and hidden.

Before this moment, they carried the weight of words and regulations, the crush of cruelty and barking orders that hounded them from place to place.

Life slipped through their fingers as they tried to hang on, to hold on. They are weary from moving without ever really arriving.

No one has ever asked them to stay.

Home is never-never land. These are women forever on the move. The powers tell them: move along, pull up your life, and just keep going. Do not stop. Not here and not now. These two women have kept moving to keep alive. There are many other women who keep moving along the fast lane in order to feel alive. For each and for all, stillness is the moment of freedom.

Stillness is the border between who you were and someone you have yet to meet.

On the other side of stillness is the vast space of uncertainty. Whom will I meet? Will they welcome me or will they walk away? Will they tell me to move on?

Still.

Still. The still small voices whisper to the woman. "Or maybe someone will look me in the face, and will tell me I am beautiful beyond all words. Perhaps someone will tell me that my children will be treasured by the nation. Perhaps someone will look upon us and see that we are good."

Still.

Still.

The women know the pieces of their lives are being gathered up. They are still here.

They are still ready to walk toward the borders that nations have constructed between the insiders and outsiders. These are the borders where people wait and wait to the sound of muzak and the shuffling of papers. There is no stillness in this waiting.

The two women recognize each other in the lineup at the border. Are you still here?

Yes, I'm still here.

Refugees are those who live along borders, who cross borders perhaps several times. They have learned to think along borders, to hope and believe along borders. It is this existence that makes them especially threatening in a time when many nation-states are worried that they are losing control of their borders.

In the greedy age of globalization, the borders of every nation-state are being erased. Money and communications whirl around the world, pass in and out and around borders without check. Many governments feel increasingly helpless in the face of these silent and unseen invasions of their sovereignty.

This is the context in which refugees have become the scapegoat for the fear that we are losing control of our borders. If we cannot stop the flow of global capital and the power of multinational corporations, we can still try to control the flow of people into our countries.

Refugees are the first to know when the border becomes a wall. They know when a border can be used to exclude.

The question of borders and boundaries is significant, not

only in the political world but in the personal world as well. There can be no identity without some kind of boundary. Feminist thinkers have articulated this in powerful and persuasive ways. Without sufficient boundaries, a person is at the mercy of another. So too, without some kind of boundaries, a nation-state will lose its sovereignty and become the colony of some greater power. Nevertheless, the crucial question then becomes whether a boundary is set by what or whom it is against or by what or whom it is for. A person with a strong sense of self, a true center, will set boundaries in ways that do not exclude others. A nation that has a vibrant sense of core values will have boundaries that will include those who share in those values. Excluding those who are different will not help a nation sustain its core values. Thus, a boundary can become a bridge or a barrier.

As I lived with those who were very different from me, I became aware of the profound differences between us, that there were borders and boundaries even within a small house. However, I also learned that these were places of meeting, that it was a good place to live.

I also realized that it was important to begin to think and imagine along these borders. Some writers have now called this "border thinking." I would say that it means learning to think in terms of AND rather than EITHER/OR. It also involves the method articulated by Thomas Aquinas: we must distinguish in order to unite.

Chapter 7

THE SAMARITAN CHURCH

The Point of the Church

Many years ago I was part of a small peace mission that went to Moscow. One of the members of that mission was the leader of a large mainline Protestant church. During a time when our movements were severely restricted by the KGB, we had time to talk with each other. He talked about the large national and international meetings in which his church had dealt with difficult issues: inclusive language, the ordination of women, the inclusion of gays and lesbians, corporate responsibility, racism within the church, and so on. He was very proud of his church's willingness to discuss these issues and to take a stand. However, he said somewhat wistfully, "I think that in talking about all these issues we've lost sight of why we are a church, and so we've lost a lot of energy."

I do not think his church is the only one in this situation. The discussion of difficult issues involving *how* to solve problems requires a fundamental attunement to the Spirit of Christ, of the *why* of it all. If my experience at Romero House has taught me anything it is that it is in drawing close to the deep suffering of others that we will find joy, we will find Christ alive, between us and among us. Once we remove ourselves from this neighborly relationship, all the discussions about issues and problems in the churches become dust and ashes.

We pray together each day at Romero House. We pray because we must, because the burdens that we share and the blessings that are given are too much for our little hearts and minds. Our prayer is not very creative, but it is consistent, and it is real. We have a monthly celebration of the Eucharist, and many of us know that the present form of the Eucharist is not as inclusive as we would want. Nevertheless, we cannot wait for the perfect sacrament in order to celebrate the Eucharist. We need to be nourished; we need a way to join our small thanksgivings to the longer and deeper thanksgiving of Jesus. We need a way of uniting our small local community to the wider and longer community of the church. It is at the Eucharist that we experience the local and the global as one.

Prayer becomes an urgent necessity when you are face to face with great suffering and need. The stranger summons us to become responsible and strong, but we know how weak we are, how weary with the vast indifference of the systems that we work in. It is the other who summons us not only to action but also to prayer.

And it is the one in great need who summons us to become what Salvadoran theologian Jon Sobrino S.J. calls "The Samaritan Church." When Jesus was asked "Who is my neighbor?" he responded that it was the one who drew near to the man by the side of the road, who saw him, who was faced by him, who then took him to the inn and stayed with him.

This story becomes forever the paradigm of Christian discipleship. It is within the reach of mercy that we become Christian. There are many courses and articles on ministry in the church, and they are important. However, they also tend to rely heavily on a professional model of training and competence. The minister can become the consultant, the facilitator, the organizer, the counselor. These can be valuable forms of service, but if they are removed from the cry of suffering people, they can miss the point and purpose of it all.

The significance of the Samaritan church is a central theme in Don DeLillo's masterful book *Underworld*. Arguably one of the finest contemporary novels in America, it is situated in the Cold War period that shaped the United States from 1950 to 1990. The cover of the book, designed before 9/11, is eerily prescient: it depicts the skyline of New York City with the twin towers dominating the background and a plane flying close to them. In the foreground is a small church, a very ugly old church. Within the pages of the novel we learn that this is the home base for a group of friars and nuns who go out every day to feed those in the underground of the city, the people who live in subways, the graffiti artists who paint pictures to remember the death of those who would otherwise remain invisible. This is the contemporary image of the church of the catacombs, the church formed in the abandoned places of empire.

I am not suggesting that everyone should go out and work in soup kitchens. There is a variety of gifts within the church, and the Spirit calls in many and different ways. However, I am suggesting that the works of mercy must be given a privileged place within our church community. Within this reach of mercy the desire for justice will become true and real and constant. Within this reach of mercy, we will learn the meaning of the great commandment to love our neighbor. This is the most important thing we need to learn in order to become disciples of Jesus.

The invitation to become a good neighbor, to live beyond the forced opposites of friends or enemies, is open to all of us—clergy, religious, and laity. Indeed, it is an invitation that makes all of these churchy categories somewhat secondary. Perhaps there is only one distinction that matters: those who are learning to love their neighbors and those who remain indifferent to them.

The weaknesses of the church, of each of us, are usually quite obvious. It is rather remarkable how accepting people are of most of these weaknesses. However, I think there is one weakness that people cannot accept and that is indifference to suffering. The church that walks by the one suffering by the side of the road has nothing significant to say about the meaning of the gospel.

"I Also Am the Church"

However, the church is not simply out there and up there. It is within each of us, within the reach of each of us. A refugee from Rwanda taught me this most important lesson at one of our Romero House liturgies.

One of the readings from the Scriptures that Sunday was the story in which Moses tries to pray for his people, but his arms begin to flag. In this story, Aaron goes to assist him, holding up the arms of Moses so he can continue in prayer.

Augustin from Rwanda was particularly pensive. It was 1994, and he had barely escaped with his wife and children from the genocide in his country, but many cousins, brothers, and sisters had been murdered. The horror of this news had been compounded by reports that some members of the Catholic clergy had encouraged the genocide or at least remained silent.

"When I think about what happened in my country," he said, "I think that the church must have got tired and stopped praying. And I am very sad. It makes me question my faith. But then I remember that I am also the church, and I must, like Aaron, help the church hold up its hands and pray. And so I must ask myself what I have done to help the church pray and become holy and just. The church is not just the priests; it is each of us helping each other become holy."

In the city where I live, the local church has the memory of a time when it was profoundly shaped by responding to the Irish refugees who arrived on its shores during the time of the great famine. Those who survived the voyage were afflicted with dangerous and contagious diseases. They were put in sheds and ignored by most of the general population, who thought they were quite dangerous. Nevertheless, groups of sisters and priests went to these warehouses to help feed and clothe those who had arrived in such desperate condition. Priests moved among the sick to administer the last rites. Many of these priests and sisters became ill in the process. The young, forty-three-year-old bishop at the time, Michael Power, died because he reached out to the people in the warehouses. It was a noble time, a time of great authenticity. Later, the church would build schools and universities, large hospitals and social agencies. Later, there would be questions about the meaning and purpose of the church. The statue pictured on the cover of this book, taken from a park named in honor of these Irish refugees, manifests their hope and depicts their summons to the church to become a Samaritan church.

The Church by the Side of the Road

Let us return to the parable of the Good Samaritan. It is possible to enter into this story from many directions. I have described the church as the Good Samaritan. However, it is also possible, even probable, that the church is also like the person by the side of the road. It has been beaten and robbed, and the assault and theft have taken place by those within the church who have abused their power and authority. The church in the United States and Canada has been severely humiliated and weakened by the revelations of sexual abuse and the subsequent cover-up of this abuse. It has been cast by the side of the road.

It is a time of great humiliation. It is a great fall for the Catholic Church that has achieved enormous power in Canada and the United States. The church has many properties and great wealth, at least on paper.

Yet these are the trappings of power. It becomes clearer with each passing day that, although the church may have authority, it no longer has power. It issues statements that few listen to. This is an immense tragedy because the statements are thoughtful and, sometimes, even prophetic.

The church has been humiliated, has grown weary, and can no longer lift its arms in prayer. This is the time when it must listen to the wisdom of someone like Augustin, the voice of the stranger among us, the voice of one who has suffered and who has seen. It is a time when the church needs to allow itself to be cared for by those who want it to become strong again.

I recall giving a talk to a large group of church administrators. It was one of the strangest experiences I have ever had. When I walked into the dining room, no one looked up, and no one was talking with anyone. As people filed into the large hall for the lecture, they sat side by side, looking ahead, looking down, silently. I realized that the people in this group were totally depressed. These were the people who had to bear the burden of all the consequences of the scandals in the church. They could not be Samaritans. They were beaten and bowed down by the side of the road.

The present situation of the church is poignantly depicted by the artist Hugo Simberg in his painting *The Wounded Angel*. The painter himself has never explained the meaning of *The Wounded Angel*, but it has evoked many interpretations. The painting depicts an angel with a bandaged head, blindfolded in a way, sitting on a stretcher, bowed down and beaten. She is being carried by two simple peasant boys. If you look closely, you see that she is being carried outside the city.

One possible interpretation is that the wounded angel is the church. We do not know who has wounded her or why, but she is beaten and suffering. Nevertheless, the poor are carrying her, the church, outside the city—away from the place of power and influence so that the wounded angel can live among the poor and be healed. It is those who are poor who need, more than anyone, for the church to become good and merciful again. It is through the poor who cannot afford not to hope that the church may be healed. Middle-class Christians can afford to engage in what the feminist ethicist Sharon Welch calls "the ideology of cultured despair." We can afford to despair because our lives are not totally wrecked by the present situation in the world. We can afford to give up on the church. However, for those on the margins of this society, this kind of despair can mean death. They cannot afford not to hope in the church.

Let us note that the Samaritan who cares for the wounded one is the stranger and foreigner. In this story, as in the story of the Canaanite woman, It is the one who is different who cares for those of us who are strange and in need. This is an important insight that eluded Emmanuel Levinas. He was so insistent that the other can command us to become ethical, that the other summons us to be ourselves, that he did not realize that we too are "other" and in need. This means that our great need can summon others to be good and responsible.

Levinas was so committed to ensuring that the difference and the demand of the other be respected that he created a rather frozen paradigm—in which the other always remained completely other. In my experience, as we live together with people who are different from ourselves, the possibility of becoming neighbors emerges. The neighbor is neither the same as we are nor totally different. Becoming a neighbor allows for a difference without indifference.

To acknowledge that we as a church are in need of a Good

Samaritan is to recognize that we can find our way forward to our true selves if we listen to the call of the stranger. The stranger may be a person, another culture, another religion, a different social class. The stranger is the one who calls us home.

To acknowledge the beaten-down reality of our church is also, paradoxically, to recognize the true word that the church has to speak within the culture. The church could and should say to the political and social leaders of our country: we too were once proud and powerful; we too were once listened to and respected; we too were once the center of our particular world. Now we have been humiliated; we have become powerless and without influence. Nevertheless, we still have the capacity to do good. We have let go of the illusions of greatness so that we can be good once again.

Let us end the consultations and the planning and the renovation of buildings and programs. And let us as a church go and live outside the city and take refuge among those who are the strangers. Let us let them welcome us; and there we shall be healed.

The Authoritative Witness

When Paul Tillich first articulated the "method of correlation," he was living in difficult times. At the risk of oversimplifying, he said that the task of theology was to attend to the questions posed by a culture or context and then to correlate these to the message of the scriptures. Much easier said than done, as David Tracy has argued in his *Blessed Rage for Order*. Nevertheless, for all their differences, both Tillich and Tracy still demonstrate enduring confidence in the power of texts, the message itself.

As I listen to many young people today, who are immersed in the sufferings and anxieties of their age, I hear that it is difficult for them to believe in any text as authoritative, any person as authoritative. "We listen to what the church leaders say," they say, "but then we see how they live, and we don't believe what they say."

Ultimately, the preaching of the good news today will have to rely primarily on the text of lives, on the witness of those whose lives give weight to their words. There is no shortcut, no easier way to make "sense" of the gospel message.

In the midst of the dissatisfied cravings of this culture, the witness of people living with gratitude, with a joyful sense of having enough, of being enough, is a powerful statement.

In the midst of weakening structures of political meaning and purpose, the testimony of those who nevertheless have a sense of meaning and purpose is powerful, persuasive.

In the midst of the clutter and fragmentation of the times, the witness of lives that are concentrated and whole is simply eloquent.

This is to live joyfully in the midst of the particular suffering of our time and place, and it is always the surest sign of the gospel—it is persuasive; it makes sense.

Acknowledgments

This book became possible because of the immense support and encouragement of many people.

I thank John Fraser, the Master of Massey College, and his wife and best friend, Elizabeth MacCallum, who provided a warm welcome at Massey College during 2008–2009 when I was a senior resident there. Together with Anna Luengo, the administrator of the College, and many junior and senior fellows, they provided the space and time for me to do a sustained reading of some of the continental thinkers who have pondered the summons of the stranger.

The members of the Romero House community, the board, staff, interns, residents, and neighbors covered many bases to provide me with the time to write. I am particularly grateful to Heather White and Sarah Villiger, who generously took on more leadership during this period.

As always, my agent, Lee Davis Creal, provided wise advice. Michael Leach of Orbis Books suggested the initial idea of this book and skillfully nudged it toward completion.

Notes on Sources
and Recommended Readings

Introduction

Some of the stories relating to Romero House appeared in an earlier version in my book *At the Border Called Hope: Where Refugees Are Neighbors.* However, that book focused more on the social and political realities of the lives of refugees. *The Other Face of God* moves to a deeper level of theological reflection.

I have found some of the contemporary French postmodern thinkers particularly helpful in thinking through the summons of the stranger. Most of these writers are insider/outsiders, that is, from minority groups or former colonies of the French empire.

My indebtedness to Emmanuel Levinas, the Jewish French philosopher, will be evident throughout this book—particularly his reflections on the Face and the Summons. His major works, *Totality and Infinity* and *Otherwise Than Being*, are difficult and demanding but well worth the effort. A series of interviews with Levinas (conducted by Philippe Nemo) are more accessible and are published as *Ethics and Infinity.*

While I have a profound respect for the emphasis Levinas places on the face-to-face encounter, I have come to see that his emphasis on the "asymmetrical" quality of the relationship seems like a frozen paradigm. He insists that our responsibility for the other is greater than the responsibility of the other for us. In his efforts to claim a priority for the needs of the stranger, he does not account for the shifts in that relationship as people relate to each other over a long period of time. In Chapter 4, I emphasize that strangers can become neighbors.

A moving tribute to Levinas was published by his friend Jacques Derrida as *Adieu*. Derrida's reflections, like those of Levinas, reflect the sensibility of an insider/outsider in France today. See Derrida's reflection *Of Hospitality*. Here and elsewhere he discusses "impasses," such as the fact that the demand for absolute altruism can never be assuaged, can never be fulfilled. Simon Critchley provides a helpful survey of more recent continental thinking on ethics in his *Infinitely Demanding: Ethics of Commitment, Politics of Resistance*.

The one French writer I have chosen not to rely on is Julia Kristeva. She has written an important book titled *Stranger to Ourselves* in which she argues that we reject strangers because we reject the unknown and threatening parts of ourselves. This presumes that the unknown is threatening. It can also be promising.

For an excellent summary of ethical considerations involving the stranger, see Terry Eagleton's *Trouble with Strangers: A Study of Ethics*.

As always I am indebted to Hannah Arendt's fresh insights into the political and religious significance of "natality," the fact that with each new child a fresh world comes into being. She wrote about this most succinctly in her *The Human Condition.*

Chapter 1
The Summons

The dynamic relationship between mercy and justice is laid out in a foundational way in *The Principle of Mercy* by Jon Sobrino S.J. I am indebted to Kathleen McAlpin R.S.M., who first introduced me to this understanding of mercy. Her reflections were published as *Ministry That Transforms*, a book that presents a contemplative model of theological reflection based on sessions that she held for the Romero House interns over the course of a year.

My reflections titled "When the Stranger Summons" were initially published in *New Theology Review.*

The quotation regarding the summons of the earth is found in *Arctic Dreams* by Barry Lopez, xix–xx.

Chapter 2
The Empire of the Self

For a more detailed presentation of the American empire see my *Reweaving Religious Life: Beyond the Liberal Model* (chap. 1) and *Radical Gratitude* (chap. 5). Chalmers Johnson's *Blowback* and *The Sorrows of Empire* give a vivid description of the reach of empire in its more pernicious aspects. For a more sober assessment of the challenges of the future, see Fareed Zakaria's *The Post-American World.* Although most writers make the assessment that America will not be the center of the world for much longer, there are also those who have more faith in America's ability to reinvent itself. See *Are We Rome?* by Cullen Murphy and *The Future of Power*, by Joseph Nye.

Tony Judt's *Ill Fares the Land* was written shortly before his death. It presents a clarion call to reclaim a politics that cares for the needs of strangers. The quotation is from page 217. Reinhold Niebuhr articulated the inherent ambiguities of power in *The Irony of History*.

James Finlay's *Merton's Palace of Nowhere* is the best presentation of Merton's distinction between the true self and the false self and the various ramifications of this distinction. The quote from Merton is taken from his classic *New Seeds of Contemplation*, page 47.

For an important psychological discussion of self-centeredness, see Christopher Lasch's *The Culture of Narcissism* and *The Minimal Self*. Interestingly enough, Lasch argues that this narcissism is linked to the loss of boundaries between the self and the world. On the one hand, the self projects its needs and wants onto the world; on the other hand, the realities of the needs of the world can crash in upon the self because of a lack of boundaries.

Chapter 3
The Concentrated Life

Robert Bellah's reflections on the importance of finding the cultural alternatives within a culture can he found in his *Habits of the Heart: Individualism and Commitment in American*

Life. Wendell Berry's early writings on location and local knowledge are collected in *The Art of the Commonplace.* His later, and more political, insights are collected in his *Citizenship Papers.* The intriguing insight into the significance of focal things and focal practices in a postmodern context are articulated by Albert Borgmann in his *Technology and the Character of Contemporary Life.*

Chapter 4
The God of Small Neighborhoods

The two most helpful thinkers on the question of neighborhoods are Wendell Berry and Jane Jacobs. Berry writes from a rural and homogenous perspective, whereas Jacobs reflects on a diverse urban context. Most of Berry's key writings can be found in two collections of his essays: *The Art of the Commonplace* and *Citizenship Papers.* The quote on community in this chapter is taken from his novel *Jayber Crow.* His reflections on local knowledge can be found online as *Local Knowledge in the Age of Informmation.* Jane Jacobs's classic work is *The Death and Life of Great American Cities,* a book that has influenced a whole generation of urban thinkers. Originally an American, she fled to Toronto during the Vietnam War and was the most influential person in shaping Toronto's approach to neighborhoods. The French Jesuit thinker Michel de Certeau (*The Practice of Everyday Life*) has also looked at cities and institutions from below. His distinction between strategies developed from above and tactics that people employ from below is interesting and helpful.

The Neighbor: Three Inquiries in Political Theology by Slavoj Zizek, Eric L. Santner, and Kenneth Reinhard presents some new perspectives for political theology. The quotation is from page 16.

This emphasis on place and neighborhood is very countercultural. For two important books on the loss of place, see *No Sense of Place* by Joshua Meyerowitz and *Elsewhere USA* by Dalton Conley.

I recommend *Apocalypse and Allegiance: Worship, Politics, and Devotion in the Book of Revelation* by J. Nelson Kraybill as a fine resource on the imperial context of the early church.

Chapter 5
Systems without a Face;
Files without a Name

I have used Hannah Arendt as my major resource on the realities of systematic evil. This was initially and most fully developed in her classic *The Origins of Totalitarianism*. A restatement of her insights in terms of contemporary organizations is chillingly presented by Earl Shorris in his *The Oppressed Middle*.

Chapter 6
The In-Between Christ

In chapter 4 of my *Radical Gratitude* I more fully develop the notion of power as the energy in between people. These considerations of the Holy Spirit as the power in the in-between spaces and places flows from that. An excellent and early articulation of this can be found in *The Go-Between God: The Holy Spirit and the Christian Mission* by John V. Taylor.

Miroslav Volf has explored issues of identity and difference in his masterly *Exclusion and Embrace: A Theological Exploration of Identity, Otherness, and Reconciliation.* Volf is writing out of the painful awareness of the Croatian Serbian conflict. Volf uses Paul G. Heibert's insight that identity involves focusing on the center rather than on maintaining a boundary. See 71n.

The key reference on "border thinking" is Walter T. Mignolo's *Local Histories/Global Designs.* Other thinkers exploring the kind of thinking that sustains differences are Abdulheder Khatabi (a Moroccan philosopher) and Eduard Glissant.

For a good summary of the issues of boundaries in personal relationships, see *Boundaries* by Henry Cloud and John Townsend.

My meditation on Stillness originally appeared in *Holiness and the Feminine Spirit: The Art of Janet McKenzie,* edited by Susan Perry.

Chapter 7
The Samaritan Church

The phrase "The Samaritan Church" has been used by Jon Sobrino S.J. in several of his essays. For a good presentation of Sobrino's image, see "Radicalizing the Comprehensiveness of Mercy" by James F. Keenan in *Hope and Solidarity,* a collection of essays in honor of Sobrino.

William Cavanaugh has written several essays on the Eucharist as uniting the local and global with a new imagination of time and space. See his "The World in a Wager: A Geography of the Eucharist as Resistance to Globalization." Available online.

The story of the crisis of Irish refugees arriving in Toronto in 1847 has been told by Mark G. McGowan in his *Death or Canada: The Irish Famine Migration to Toronto, 1847.*

I owe to Richard Rohr OFM this particular interpretation of *The Wounded Angel.*